Crusade in Asia

Other Books by the Same Author:

I SAW THE FALL OF THE PHILIPPINES

MOTHER AMERICA

MY BROTHER AMERICANS

I SEE THE PHILIPPINES RISE

THE UNITED

Crusade in Asia

PHILIPPINE VICTORY

Carlos P. Romulo

The John Day Company   New York

TO VIRGINIA

who gave me the balance and determination needed in critical moments when I was forced to make decisions that were far-reaching and that might have cost us much, and who stood by me as helpmeet and comrade-in-arms once those decisions were made.

Foreword

OF THIS I am convinced—
Communism never wins in any land. . . .
When a government is clean, competent, honorable,
and representative of the wishes and needs of the people,
when it is the people, Communism doesn't have the ghost
of a chance.

Only when a government becomes corrupt and graft-
ridden and morally diseased is Communism able to slink
in through the back door to assume arrogant control.

It appears never as the victor, but as a scavenger and
a feaster upon corpses, and it can survive only where it
*finds food to live on—*in a country where Democracy has
died!

Crusade in Asia

Chapter I

THIS was the day we had waited and prayed and fought for in the Philippines. It was the Fourth of July, 1946.

We had chosen it as our Independence Day because it was America's, in honor of the country that for half a century had trained us in the ways of democracy and had fought with us the nightmare battle against Japan. It was a final gesture of gratitude toward a mother nation that had treated us with courtesy and that today was delivering the gift of freedom to a small country on the western rim of Asia.

After this day we would no longer be the Philippine Commonwealth. We would be an independent nation—the first in Asia to reach that longed-for goal since the war.

Over two hundred thousand people were gathered on the Luneta in the heart of Manila to watch the first Independence Day ceremonies and hear our new nation's first President, Manuel Roxas, take his oath of office. It seemed to me that everyone I had ever known and the entire history of my country were in that parklike setting. There were people from all over the Islands and from America, there were our Filipino representatives and American leaders flown over from Washington. There were men

3

and women and children who to me, personally, were the story of my life—relatives, neighbors, old friends. There were men I had gone to school with, worked with in newspaper days, worked with in legislative halls in Manila and Washington, fought beside in the Battle of the Philippines.

Above all, for me, there was my wife Virginia, from whom I had been separated by war.

In the crowd could be seen many left maimed, blinded, or scarred. There were men who wore with pride the tattered uniforms they had worn as veterans of the Revolution against Spain, or on Bataan or Corregidor, and others, mostly women, in the sombre attire of mourning.

But every face wore the look of hope, too much for the heart to hold.

This was our day. After this, we would be free.

Paul V. McNutt, speaking for America, read the proclamation of Philippine Independence, signed by Harry S. Truman, President of the United States. General Douglas MacArthur was given an ovation equal to the one given President Roxas. His eagle look did not change, but it was apparent he was greatly moved. He too had waited and worked and fought for this day. The blueprint for it had been drawn when his father, General Arthur MacArthur, as our military governor, had instituted in the Philippines the writ of habeas corpus, one of the cornerstones of the Bill of Rights. The groundwork had been laid when Fil-American forces fought with MacArthur, the son, to hold the Philippines. I watched him as he stood, head up, hand to forehead, looking over the crowded Luneta as calmly as he had stood out on the bared rock of Corregidor to count the Japanese planes overhead, and I thought: "A great man! Nothing can ever tear him down!"

His comment on the day would be made to me later. "Carlos, America buried imperialism here today!"

Roxas was speaking. Listening to him, I thought of Manuel Luis Quezon, our leader in the fight for independence, who had not lived to see this day of culmination. Quezon had died in exile in the United States as President of the Philippine Commonwealth, in 1944, while our country was still held by the Japanese. At his death Vice President Sergio Osmeña, scholarly, serious, and a splendid statesman, had automatically become President. Now Roxas, elected in November, 1945, was solemnly voicing the words that made him the first President of the Philippine nation, and in him we had a worthy successor to all the other Filipino leaders who had helped our country on its way to freedom.

Roxas had taken an active and aggressive part in politics in Manila before the war. He had served as a brigadier general in the United States Army with MacArthur on Corregidor. I had come to know him in those endless days and nights when, to escape the tunnel for a breath of fresh air, we had sat out on rocks overlooking the bay and talked above the crash of bombs about the future of the Philippines, when war ended and our side had won—for we had been certain even then that democracy would be victor. We had made great plans on that shattered rock for the future of a country undergoing as terrible an ordeal as any country has ever known, and survived.

Quezon had been rescued from the Rock. MacArthur had been forced to leave. Roxas had been ordered to remain and face the Japanese. He resisted every attempt on their part to make him an official. He had used the excuse that he had once had tuberculosis.

Certainly on this day he looked like a man in the prime of life. I listened to him pledging himself to the service of his country and knew that all those plans he had made under bombings would come to reality, and that the Philippines was coming of age under the guiding hand of a great and worthy leader.

He had a fine grasp of all the country's needs, and they were many and pressing. Directly after his election he had gone to the United States, and in Washington, before the board of the Export and Import Bank, he had answered for two hours the questions fired at him on the economic status of the Philippines. I had been amazed at the able way he had answered them all. As a result, Filipino prestige had been enhanced in the eyes of the hard-headed American financiers and economists, and it was clear that this man, who before becoming President had been able to secure additional aid from the United States, was the man among men who would be able to pull the Philippines out of the postwar morass.

It was indeed a morass. I looked around the Luneta at our great beautiful city, mellowed by antiquity, scarred by war. Wherever one looked was rubble and devastation. Many of our magnificent churches, centuries old, our costly modern buildings, our beautiful homes, that had helped to make the city of Manila famed around the earth as "the Pearl of the Orient," had been blasted into dust by Japanese bombs.

But everywhere, on the face of the people, on the face of the land, was a look of newness and hope.

Over on Bataan, trees grew again in soil that had been soaked with American and Filipino blood. Corregidor shone in the sun, a mighty rampart rising out of Manila Bay, with no reminder there of the tunnels within where Filipino and American soldiers had huddled together in a miasma of gangrene, dysentery, and slime. Manila Bay dimpled in the sun, showing no trace of the liquid death showered down from the planes of the Rising Sun. Peace had returned to the Philippines, and with it the long-pledged boon of freedom, and if there were invisible wounds on our land and its people, they were like our honored dead; they were with us, but apparent only to our inner eyes.

Otherwise, flowers bloomed on the Luneta, voices broke with cheering, speeches were made, and bands played, while the two flags, Filipino and American, waved together for the last time over Philippine soil.

There was too much for the eye to see, the heart to hold. I thought back over the long struggle that had brought us to this day. Deep in the Filipino soul is the passion for freedom. Conflict and war had written no new chapters in our history. They are our heritage. Ours has been a history of struggle from earliest times, and always the struggle was an assertion of passionate faith in the principle that all men are born free.

That is why we have understood America. That is why we fought against, and with, America.

In ages beyond the ken of history the Filipinos had fought in this faith, and always against fearful odds. There

7

had been the unyielding struggle against Imperial Spain, then against the conqueror America, then with America against the aggressor Japan. The struggle had heightened within the swift-moving first half of the twentieth century, and the goal had come nearer, and still we had fought on, in legislative halls and around diplomatic tables, and always for freedom. We had developed great leaders, and lost them, and others had sprung to take their place. We had been given the best advice, care, and guidance America could give. And then, with the end in sight, we had been forced to fight again in the field against a juggernaut Japan that had found our little country the single victim of its aggression which would not be conquered, and which alone, in all Asia, had stood side by side with America.

I looked out over the crowd and thought with a full heart: A nation of heroes, and of heroines, who never stopped fighting!

Blinking, I looked up into the sky. It was as clear as it had been the morning after the attack on Pearl Harbor, when from the balcony of the Herald building I had stood with Cela, the newspaper's office cat, pressing worriedly between my feet as the first Japanese planes roared down in perfect formation over Manila. The day before, they had bombed Camp John Hay and Clark Field, and our planes—our beautiful American planes—had been caught like sitting pigeons on the ground.

I felt my throat thicken. I can still get sick with the hopeless despair we had known in those days as the Fil-Americans had fought back without planes, without guns, ammunition, food, or medical care against an enemy that had poured death down over us from this sky without ceasing. How the Japanese had hated us, their fellow Orientals who had sided with the white men! They had made us pay, then and after. I felt again that illness of despair in the midst of the cheering and the speeches and the brave new hopes, and for a moment fought for control, telling myself it was over, all over there was no shadow on our sky. . . .

I did not know

No one knew. No one on the Luneta on this brave day could have dreamed that within two years our good Roxas would be dead and that we of the Philippines would be launched on our fourth fight for freedom, the most terrifying of all because it would be a war of intangibility, waged against shadows.

On this day I would have said anyone was crazy who hinted that such a Christian and democratic country as ours could ever be infested with an ideology crawling toward us from the other side of Asia. Communism was a word that belonged in Russia. Russia had been an ally on our side in the war. The war was over, we had earned our independence, and what hold could any Russian ideology have on the minds of free men!

Years after this day I would still be scoffing at any suggestion of a serious Communistic infiltration in the Philippines. In this, I was not alone. By the time we stopped scoffing, it was almost too late.

For despite the fact that as a Filipino delegate to the United Nations in San Francisco I had seen the Russian delegates in action and been made uneasy by their truculence, still I saw no reason to fear Russia. We had no concept at this time of Russian power. We had no premonition then that in so short a time China—mighty China—was to fall under the hammer and sickle, and that once again the shadow of aggression would be cast over the Philippines.

We had not known, when in San Francisco we wrote the Charter of the United Nations, that an atom bomb had been created. We wrote that charter on the basis of conventional armament. When the bomb exploded at Hiroshima it made obsolete many of the plans of the United Nations.

All this, like the death of Roxas, lay in the future. We did not know what lay ahead on July 4, 1946. We were certain only that the line we planned to follow would be in the American way.

With paralyzing suddenness that way would open before us and reveal both bitterness and glory. Within the next few swift-moving years we were to relive in the Philippines the entire history of America. The pictures of Washington and Lincoln that hung on our schoolroom walls would be replaced with pictures of Quezon, who was to us our George Washington, and of the man we would find for our own Abraham Lincoln, of and for the people, when the need came.

We would have, also, our Harding and Dougherty, our Teapot Dome. Yes, we were to relive America's story in complete detail, even to our own Alger Hiss. But on this day of independence there was no shadow on our sky. Yet we did know that what lay ahead would not be easy.

It is difficult for any country that has been dependent

to stand alone. In the Philippines we were assuming independence on the heels of a devastating war.

Around us our beautiful capital lay in ruins. Seventy per cent of Manila was wreckage. Our public buildings and our records were destroyed. Business had ebbed to the vanishing point, and down at the bottom of Manila Bay lay our country's millions—the gold and silver coinage we ourselves had sunk there after burning the paper money, to keep it from the hands of the Japanese during the siege of the Philippines.

Even worse than the stripping of our resources was the moral trauma that follows war. To survive, men had been forced to kill, maraud, steal, lie, slink about by night and hide in the hills by day. Families had been broken up or completely destroyed. Children had been trained to steal, lie, and conceal to save their own or their parents' lives. For a time, morality had almost been blasted out of existence by the enemy fire.

Now guns were forbidden by law, but it still seemed that almost everyone went armed, some for purposes of defense, but many for offense. Many of the bands of defenders who had fought against the Japanese were refusing to turn in their arms. They had come to like their bandit existence, and we had no idea how many were still hiding out in the hills.

To reestablish law and order in the Philippines would be in itself a task for giants. And this was only a small part of the work that must go into the making of a working independence.

I looked out over the ruins of our great beautiful city and at faces scarred with war and shining with hope, and thought of the struggle and poverty and disappointment that must lie ahead. No, it would not be easy. It would mean one more fight by our tiny nation.

Only this time it would be different. This time we would be free!

There was a silence all over the park and everyone was on his feet. The sky clouded and a light rain began to fall. I saw MacArthur standing with his hand in snappy military salute. Then we were all watching the American flag come down slowly from its place against the sky, and in its stead, slowly, rose the flag of the Philippines. All around us in that crowded park there was the sound of weeping, and I do not think there was a face in all that crowd— American or Malayan—that was not touched by emotion.

Slowly and at the same pace the two flags were moving, the red-white-and-blue with its stripes and stars coming down, the red-white-and-blue with its sun and three stars rising; and just as it reached the top, by one of those odd tricks of tropical weather the rain stopped as suddenly as if a tap had been turned off, the sun burst through the clouds at the exact moment the flag stopped its upward climb, and there it flung itself out in a sudden blaze of color—the flag of the Republic of the Philippines —against a brightly shining sky.

This was farewell to America in the Philippines. This was hail and farewell to a flag we Filipinos had fought to hold over the Philippines, and many had died defending it against the Japanese. This was our reward. This was the symbol of freedom—the abdication of one proud flag for another. The Filipino flag against the sky marked the end of the long dream that had obsessed our lives, and the lives before us of our fathers, and grandfathers, and who could say how many more?

I was seeing the Philippines rise again, and this time, truly free.

It was one of history's significant moments. Freedom had come to a little Oriental country on the rim of Asia. It had been handed down to us from Runnymede by the Magna Charta of 1215; from Philadelphia's Declaration of Independence in 1776; from the walls of the Bastille in Paris in 1789; from the bloodied field of Gettysburg in 1863 where first the immortal words were spoken: "Government of the people, by the people, and for the people . . ."

Now these words became part of Asia.

We had earned them at Bataan, a few miles away, at Corregidor, standing stalwart in the bay. The Filipinos had won them in battle; with these words, we were assuming the role of a democratic independent nation in the Far East.

I knew in that first moment when our flag stood alone against the Philippine sky that this was the beginning of freedom in all Asia. It was on its way, nothing could stop it from this moment on. And it was the pebble that released the avalanche; a few years later, Indonesia would be set free by the Netherlands, and India by Mother England, and what can follow but Indochina—British Malaya —Africa?

It is inevitable.

In the face of these changes, now may be the time to tell the story of the Philippines' fourth and most recent fight for freedom, and of the defenses thrown up by one of the tiniest countries in Asia when it learned that the democracy it had won was about to die. And again, I am writing in the disliked first person because to me the struggle against Communism has been a personal story, and I can tell it in no other way.

I am often asked what I was thinking in that moment when the Filipino flag was raised over the Luneta.

There were many things to think about and remember. I remembered my father, and the days when I was a small boy and he an anonymous guerrilla, hiding out to fight the hated Americans who were bent on conquering our land. I remembered the way I had quivered with childish hatred at learning that my gentle grandfather had been given the "water cure" by American soldiers. I remembered my own determination as a boy to hate Americans and all things American forever, and how individual friendships among the soldier-conquerors had won my heart, and turned my mind to American history and ideals. I had gone to school in the United States, which became my second home. I had served as MacArthur's aide in World War II. I had every reason to revere and respect the power of America.

At this time I was Resident Commissioner of the Philippines, living in Washington with my family. I would be the last Commissioner. My job ended automatically with the raising of the Filipino flag. We had flown from Washington to attend today's ceremonies and on our way our plane had stopped at Guam. There we delayed our flight for a few minutes to listen on the radio to the awesome broadcast of the Bikini atom bomb tests. The sound of the

14

blast was shocking to me for many reasons, and I knew it would create fear and hatred throughout the world. It was the voice of America with America's terrible potentialities for destruction.

Now I watched the Filipino flag fluttering against the blue Manila sky. There was no sound, no threat, in that spectacle. And I thought: "Here is the flying emblem of the imponderable power that makes America invincible. One thousand years from now, the raising of this flag will be remembered, and not the trial blast at Bikini."

That night there was a dance in Malacañan Palace, the White House of the Philippines, and the festivities did not end until the small hours. It had been a long and wonderful day, and when we returned to our rooms in the Manila Hotel I was emotionally spent. The hotel had been our finest. Social life had centered here. The MacArthurs had lived in its penthouse before Pearl Harbor. General Homma lived there during the Japanese occupation. The American flag had been torn from its roof and the flag of the Rising Sun had flown there as we had watched bitterly and helplessly from Corregidor. It had been the scene of room-to-room fighting when we retook Manila. Now those years were over, but the hotel still wore the marks of war, and much of the plumbing and many walls were gone. One section had been hastily repaired to house the foreign delegates, and the room where my wife and I were staying—having no home any more in this city that was home—had been hurriedly boarded up along one wall to hide the chasm left by shellfire.

I took one last look over the city that was still awake.

15

Bursts of fireworks still were seen and heard in the streets and down along the bay. It was a day one hated to have end; for my part, I had waited for it since boyhood.

Somewhere down in that nightbound city, in the suburbs, was a spread of ashes that once had been our beautiful home. I had seen the twisted rubble that were the skeletal remains of the newspaper office and the radio stations where I had once presided. Everything I possessed of worldly goods had been wiped out when the Japanese attacked; all by direct hits.

Nevertheless, I knew myself to be singularly blessed by God. The fact that not so much as a stick of furniture or a fragment of type remained was as nothing beside the miracle of having all my family together. We had gone separate and terrible ways during the three-and-a-half years of the Japanese occupation, and there had been many times when I had feared I would never find my wife and four sons again. In turn they had feared for me, a man with a Japanese price on his head. But the prayers had been answered and we were together.

I had chosen to live in Washington as Resident Commissioner, instead of staying on in Manila to run for the Vice Presidency as Osmeña had wished. I felt I could serve my country best on the international front.

Later, Roxas also asked me to be his Vice President. He sent my personal physician as his confidential emissary to see me in Washington and to ask me to run. Again, I refused. If I had accepted then, I would have become President of the Philippines less than two years after this first Independence Day.

But this, too, lay in the future, and that night I was

filled with exultation and content. I knew that over the rubble of Manila new beauty and traditions would grow. We were beginning over again—my country and its people.

The next morning I was appointed the Philippines' first permanent delegate to the United Nations. A few days later I flew back to the United States to continue the fight for international security on the world front.

With Roxas at the helm, the future of the Philippine Republic was secure.

Chapter II

AT first all went well.

President Roxas had his problems. These are to be expected in a country trying out new wings. In the United States I read of them without apprehension. Roxas was capable of handling them all.

There was first the sense of release and let-down that followed the three-and-a-half years of privation and suffering that had been the Filipino's share of World War II. This, added to the moral laxity born of war, gave way to many a reckless attitude toward the future. Some who received compensation for their ruined businesses or homes did not use the money at once to build again. Instead, they launched on a brief orgy of enjoying the good food, clothing, luxuries, and recreations that had not been theirs for so long a time. The after-effect was, of course, poverty again and bitterness.

Certainly this was improvident of people who had suffered so much, but they can hardly be blamed.

Roxas handled their problems with a sure, firm hand.

Matters of housing and employment and nutrition were dealt with one at a time. Meantime, other and more dangerous problems came to light.

The explosion of the atom bomb at Hiroshima ended the war in the Pacific, and with it the great war push stopped. As a result, planes, trucks, guns, material of every kind, millions of dollars worth of uninventoried goods, were lying about the country, ready for greedy hands. America had no more need for this uncounted treasure. No wonder the cupidity of certain politicians was aroused!

Manuel Roxas nipped their plans in the bud. For a time the war materiel remained virtually untouched, mountains of it, millions in treasure, unwanted, waiting. . . .

There was a more serious problem. No one knew then how serious it would be. But in this same year, 1946, that gave us our independence, Communism first showed its face boldly in the Philippines, only then we did not recognize it fully as the enemy it would prove to be. We thought of it first as an annoying disturber of the peace.

To understand the movement and the way it grew we must go back before the days of the occupation, when Americans and Filipinos suffered together in the Philippines under the Japanese heel.

Then we must go back farther than that, to the days before the war. Looking backward, I can see now how small the movement was in the beginning and how few were in at its birth. And we know now that there are always these few, and one leader who begins it all. Recognized, they can be stopped in time.

To our credit, we did recognize our first Communists, and we did stop them. But not soon enough, and not permanently. They found the crevice in our democratic armor. They crept in, and this is the story of their slow, remorseless crawling into the very heart of our nation, up to the very doors of our municipal halls. A few reached the inside.

That was when our new nation tottered. That is when we almost went under!

But I must tell it all slowly and carefully, because even now I am bewildered by the way such coups can be brought about and the means by which serious-minded men can be duped and even be made accessories to the crime of Communism.

The Communist attack when it was launched would be world-wide. I was to see it in action in Geneva, in the United States, and in the Philippines. Now, by the advantage of hindsight, I am able to see clearly the apparently innocent way it began in the Philippines—long before Pearl Harbor, long before Bataan.

In Manila, as everywhere else, the attack was launched upon—and later by—our bright young men, those to whom we were giving the best our country had to offer by way of education and opportunity, and from whom we had every reason to expect the best in return.

The net was first spread in Manila several years before the war on a purely social basis by a few of our brightest young men. One was Dr. Vicente Lava of the University of the Philippines. The other was Luis Taruc, then only a high school student and later to become our Number One Communist and public enemy to the peace of the Philippines. Others were labor leaders such as Crisanto Evangelista and Guillermo Capadocia.

Lava was an instructor and Taruc a pupil, but they were friends. They were more than that, we know now.

They were fellow travelers. Lava was a chemistry professor, a Ph.D., graduated from Columbia University in New York. There he had been an avid reader of the writings of Marx and Lenin and other radical leaders. Make no mistake, he was a brilliant man.

The young Taruc was also an ardent student of Marx and the rest, and Lava, his teacher in Communist ideas, later would serve as his advisor. Lava helped write the Communistic articles and pamphlets with which Taruc showered the Philippines, until Lava died of tuberculosis during the war. He left many pupils to carry on with the leader Taruc.

But in the early days of their association their objective was the usual Communist aim—to collect followers. Their target was the intelligentsia.

In those days before the war I was publishing newspapers and I knew what was going on in Manila, or thought I did. I knew that these two and their friends were organizing parties, apparently literary, which were given in the homes of leading Manila newspapermen and writers. Several of my editors were lured into playing host to these affairs. Literature was discussed and poetry read, and a pleasant time was had by all. Certainly the gatherings seemed innocent enough.

We would learn later that these parties were organized so that Taruc and Lava might observe and study and select young men who might be diverted into helping form Communist cells.

So, under our very eyes, cells were formed and Communism was launched in our Christian land, and we did not know.

This was the secret pattern the Communists were following everywhere in the world. Aim for the young, the potential leaders, the cream of our youth! Aim for the good-looking, educated, intelligent, the *starry-eyed!*

This is still Communism's aim today: world youth, and the corruption of that youth! And, wherever possible, the indoctrination of children!

I no longer wonder why young people fall for the Soviet propaganda. It is carefully chosen to meet their growing demands. Youth has no defenses against its subtle flattery and its promises. The young people who fall for Communism have been led into its trap by the stars in their own eyes. They are to be pitied and understood and protected, and, if possible, saved.

Why do they fall?

I know because I have seen the Communist plan put into action. I have watched the spreading of the net from Moscow to Manila, over Europe, over Asia. And in every place I have seen it catch up youngsters who are underprivileged and have reason to protest, and others who are well provided for and have brilliant careers ahead. Many are well intentioned, but before they know it, they walk the path to treason.

Why?

They are flattered.

Let us take one of these young men, an Alger Hiss of any country, and try to see without prejudice what lure Communism has to offer that can turn him against his own country and its government, and even his own parents. What is its power?

Let us study this young man of Manila, or New York.

He is, let us say, neither prosperous nor poor, but belongs to the half-world of the partially privileged. He has read Marx and Engels, Lenin and Stalin, and he knows that the world is changing.

He is told that this is his chance as an intellectual to help move forward the evolution of human freedom.

He looks back over history and sees how the world has advanced, from feudalism and the divine right of kings and through imperialism into democracy. He is told that this grand new movement risen out of Russia is destined to sweep the world, and that by joining he can insure himself a place of prominence and power on the ground floor, in the brave new world to be.

He is excited by these promises and by the cops-and-robbers fascination of belonging to the subversive and strange and new.

He sees in Communism all the glamour of the *verboten,* and youth does not like being denied anything. He likes being different, and he likes to feel that his strength is pitted against the fuddy-duddy and antiquated. He loves argument for its own sake because he is young, and Communism lends itself ideally to controversy, to dialectics and to sophistry, and it serves as a bit between the teeth of the ardent young recruit. He has probably come under its spell while in college, where he who argues longest and loudest is the campus hero, and the bright young man, fed on arguments supplied by pamphlets and newspapers from Moscow, finds himself dazzled by his own oratory and trapped by his own sophistry. The fad becomes an obsession. He believes, because he must believe, in order to argue well. In time he is regarded by his fellow students with the respect paid to a student of Marx; he is marked as one of the intelligentsia; and he inspires more than a little fear. Proselyting begins for him in earnest, and he is sent from group to group, arguing and convincing. He achieves fame beyond the campus, and he finds that other young groups of radicals know of him and are eager to hear him speak.

So, with little effort, he has achieved a heady fame. He is on the bright brave new non-greedy anti-capitalistic side, and he is head and shoulders above all the poor boobs who believe in the old stupidities. He is the campus radical. He is its Marxian.

As long as he lives, he will wear the brand of Communism. He may not care, in the beginning. It may be a long time before he begins to care, and then it may be too late.

Often enough his talk has been all sound and fury and part of the emotional upheaval of youth. Our bright young man may have in his heart none of the intent to destroy that will justify the suspicions he will have to contend against the rest of his life. He may drop his Communistic front when he finds himself out in the world and faced with the sobering need to earn an average living, and the inner need to live as an average man. Or he may find too late that he cannot. He is dedicated to Moscow.

Flattery served to bring him into the Red fold.

There may have graduated with him another young student who has also won high honors, who has taken no part in the noisy discussions, and upon whose diploma no marks indicate the courses he has taken in treachery and treason. These are not on the curricula. But he is the truly dangerous recruit. He will not waste time in talk. He is prepared to act. He has his orders and he will carry them out in secrecy, and what he does will never be known, except in Moscow.

Another and more surprising type of recruit to Communism is the man, and woman, of the privileged class, known as the Park Avenue Pink. These are wealthy persons who contribute to dubious causes on the roseate side. They are the inheritors of their wealth and lack the sobering realistic influence of having earned it themselves. That there is a social responsibility to wealth is attested to by the many libraries, hospitals, and charitable endowments set up by the very rich. The donors to the dubious causes, however, are the rich and guilt-ridden who have been convinced by Communist propagandists that Communism only will bring about equality and enhance the dignity of the individual.

This is also the lure the Communist propaganda holds for the economically depressed. It promises to the frustrated, the well-intentioned, and the would-be big shot, personal importance, equality, and a place in the sun. If they only knew! If they could only see Communism in action!

Communism does not elevate. It debases. It does not recognize the dignity of the individual. It does not recognize the individual. All is for the state. It not only arrests human freedom, it abolishes it, by enslaving body and mind.

By way of illustration, watch a Vishinsky, a Malik, a Gromyko in action as I watched them at first hand in the United Nations. You cannot help but pity them and share their fear. Under the iron exterior an automaton is jerking to wires pulled in Moscow. They do not dare to think for themselves. To think might result in error. Error would mean liquidation. They are fanatics working for a fanatic state.

If any other United Nations delegate makes an error, he faces the disapproval of his country. They face death.

We had an incident in the United Nations when a delegate complained that his motion had been "disposed of." Later he complained again, because the Russian interpreter had interpreted the words "disposed of" as "liquidated." The poor interpreter was not to blame. That was the word he knew best. It was indicative of the Russian point of view that was to raise an impassable barrier between the Soviet delegates and the other delegates who were struggling to achieve world peace.

Communism is being sold to the young as the newest step forward in the evolution of human freedom. That is error. Tragic error. The step leads down.

While the seeds of Communism were being secretly sown in the Philippines, I first became aware of the dangers of Communism on the international front. It was while the United Nations was being founded in San Francisco in 1945. The war was still going on. The Philippines was still a Commonwealth. I was there almost on sufferance, as chief delegate of the Philippines, which was not yet an independent nation. Mine was a very small voice; nevertheless, I was determined to make it heard in behalf of democracy, and I was led to believe that the delegates might welcome what I had to say.

I would soon learn that this was true with one notable exception: Russia.

Let me state at once that I went to San Francisco with the friendliest attitude toward Russia. I had admired that country since my university days, when as a student at Columbia in New York I had taken an intensive course in radical literature under the popular Professor Vladimir Simkhovitch, recently retired from Columbia, who is one of our most effective anti-Communists. I had read the teachings of Marx, I had read Turgenev and Gorky and other great dramatic writers of Russia, and I had memorized much of Leo Tolstoi, whose books I often quoted in my debates. I had followed the story of Kerensky and considered the Soviet program one of the greatest experiments in history. With the rest of the world I had admired the Russians as fighters in World War II and the colossal effort made in their defense of Stalingrad. I had resented the attacks made against the Russians while they were our allies in that war, and I, a Catholic, had even resented the attacks made by my Church, which sounded the first warnings against the Soviet. I felt the Church was being narrow-minded and fanatic in its attitude.

Up to this time I had never met any Russians, but through my studies of their history and literature I felt that I knew them well.

So it was that I arrived in San Francisco with an open mind.

I will admit now that my friendly attitude got a bad jolt on opening day.

The United Nations organizational conference began with no opening prayer.

At this time I was still Resident Commissioner of the Philippines, and accustomed to hearing an opening prayer every day in the Lower House of Congress in Washington. This seemed an abrupt and inauspicious beginning. Here were the representatives of fifty nations gathered together in the hope of achieving unity to maintain peace. Why not open so significant a meeting with prayer?

I discussed the matter with several delegates from South America. We agreed it was a serious omission. Three of the Latin Americans and myself as spokesman went into a private consultation with the late Edward R. Stettinius, Jr., then Secretary of State and Chairman of the American delegation. He was in charge of all arrangements, since America was the host nation.

I have the most pleasant memories of Stettinius at San Francisco. His was a charming and gentlemanly personality. But he was outmatched by arrogance. He answered with obvious regret our question as to why there had been no prayer.

"I too am disturbed that there is no opening prayer," he said. "I believe and the United States delegation believes that we should have one. But the Russian delegates are against us in this matter and we do not want to start off our conference with a procedural wrangle. We want concord and harmony. So I ask you, please, do not insist upon an opening prayer."

What could we do! We had to yield to the whim of Russia. It would be the first of many such yieldings.

Then I felt my first doubts. The first day of the conference had only begun and already America had given in, and in a matter basic and paramount. We were to make this a godless conference.

By whose orders?

Stalin's.

Nevertheless, when I began my first speech at San Francisco with the words, "Let us make this floor our last battlefield," I believed with all my being that it would be so.

A caucus of the chief delegates was held two days before the opening conference. It was carefully staged, by the Russians.

Delegates were milling about the hall, not having as yet been assigned to their seats, and talking in small groups in low voices. Then into the conference room rushed a whirlwind that swept the other delegates aside as if they were dust. It was Vyacheslav Molotov, chief delegate of Soviet Russia, surrounded by his bodyguards and making his presence known.

There was a rush of photographers all around this tumultuous personage. Everything else was forgotten as Molotov, with the determination of an army tank proceeding over a battlefield, made his way to the head table, where he took his seat as if by divine right and sat, under a spatter of flash bulbs, staring around him, arrogant, contemptuous, unsmiling.

There for the first time I saw the real Russia, and my impression was that this was no dignitary come in the role of peacemaker. This was the way a gangster-killer would make his appearance in some infamous dive. Molotov's swaggering entrance had pushed aside all dignity and courtesy. I found myself thinking, So this is Russian real-ism! This is the new Russia!

I was badly shocked.

No sooner was the meeting called to order than Molotov had the floor.

Now, in all international conferences it is the accepted custom that the chairman of the delegation of the host nation acts as presiding officer. Molotov, machine-gunning his demands in the voice of authority, demanded that the ban be put on that custom. Instead of the United States being left in the chair, Molotov wanted five chairmen, the heads of delegations of the Big Five, to serve in turn, alternating alphabetically.

This was a direct slap in the face of international courtesy and obviously aimed at the United States.

I could only be reminded of the comic strip "Keeping Up With The Joneses." Here was Russia, who always before had been the losing nation, defeated even by little Japan, at last placed on the winning side. Having helped in victory, Russia was now all too obviously planning to arrange peace on its own terms, and without the ability or training to understand the simplest forms of international courtesy, or the needs or desires of any other nation.

Exequiel Padilla, Foreign Minister of Mexico, a man of distinguished appearance and a remarkably fine speaker, was one of those who opposed Molotov in this surprise move, and his protest was made in beautiful, flowing language. This was something the Russian delegate could not comprehend. No sooner had Padilla taken his seat than Molotov was again on his feet claiming in the most discourteous tone that the "memorized speech" of the delegate from Mexico did not hold.

This was not only an insult, it was an obvious falsehood. Padilla had had no chance to memorize or prepare a speech, for how could anyone have foreseen that such a startling issue would come up? Molotov himself had raised it. Here was a twisting of the truth that left an opponent helpless.

So this was the new Russian doctrine! Bulldoze and bewilder, from the start.

At this point I was not only shocked, but, to put it bluntly, I was scared.

I had not intended to speak. I was a nobody—the Philippines was not yet independent. But I was so disturbed I asked for the floor and declared myself as siding with Padilla.

Molotov did not even take the trouble to answer me. He sat back in his chair studying me with silent contempt.

I sat meekly under that basilisk stare repeating to myself the words Stettinius had impressed upon us in private: "Concord and harmony." We were to maintain those at the Peace Conference, no matter what the cost.

Molotov won, of course. The delegates of half a hundred nations—the entire conference—yielded to Molotov because we were in San Francisco in the interests of peace, and we did not want to blast all chances of peace at the start.

More frightening experiences were to follow. From that day on through the next eight years, from 1945 to 1953, I would follow my course in the United Nations from San Francisco through London, New York, Geneva, and Paris with the sense of treading on dynamite. Mine was the role of the gnat buzzing about the head of the Russian bear, and I could not escape the role. I could not be silent against the sound of treachery and insolence, and I was fated to oppose each of the Russian delegates in turn, from Molotov to the late Mr. Vishinsky, finding them always cut from the same Moscow pattern—ruthless, incomprehensible to the honest and well-intentioned, and dedicated to the goal of beating down all who opposed.

My San Francisco headquarters was in the St. Francis Hotel, where the Russian delegation was also staying. I think it was the day after the caucus that I was approached in the lobby by a young man who spoke perfect English and who invited me into the bar for a drink. He explained he was attached to the Russian delegation and he was interested in knowing if I planned to attend a party Molotov was giving in the hotel; he knew I had been invited. He pressed me to attend, and I promised to go. I could not help but be curious about meeting Molotov at first hand.

The young Russian talked of the Filipinos and the fight we had put up on Bataan. He seemed to know a great deal about us. He had read my book, *I Saw the Fall of the Philippines*. He had many questions to ask. I recall the first: "Isn't it true that the Americans practically abandoned you in the Philippines?"

I said quickly, "Not abandoned! They were outnumbered."

He mentioned the blacked-out spaces in my book where certain words and passages had been deleted. I pointed out that the book had been published in wartime when there must always be strict censorship and the War Department had used caution.

"Probably," he remarked carelessly, "those were references to the brown men fighting against the whites which the Americans did not want revealed."

The talk made me a little uneasy, but I assured him that he was wrong and that the deleted statements were of a nature that would not have been a help to our war effort, for which purpose the book had been written.

It was always "we," I noticed, when he spoke. He did not seem to think of himself as an entity and it was always a mass conviction that he voiced, as if he had no opinions of his own. Suspicion dawned in me that he had been appointed by the Russian delegation to serve as liaison officer with our Philippine delegation. He did not admit this, then or later, but all his conversation pointed that way.

I excused myself and got away, determined to avoid him from then on. Unfortunately, I had happened to mention that I always rose early, and he had instantly remarked that he too was an early riser. Every morning after this, for a week, he was in the coffee shop when I entered, hovering about, and making every excuse to join me at my table.

I began to recognize a recurrent theme in our conversations. It was the hatred of Russia for America. He would pursue the racial problems at every turn. The Negro's lot was always at the tip of his tongue and it was his answer to all pro-American argument. "Those poor people," he would say. "Do you not pity them?"

Then he would drop in a remark like this: "Of course the United States isn't really giving you Filipinos your independence. They're just playing along with the Cuban sugar interests."

And he would make the suggestion I was to have impressed upon me by every Russian I met in the United Nations in the succeeding years: "You Filipinos belong on our side. You belong with Asia, not with the Americans."

One morning he dropped a casual remark: "Since you are planning to vote for the admission of Argentina . . ."

These words alarmed me. The question of Argentina's membership had become a controversial item, exploited by the Soviet delegation in its drive to secure membership for the Ukraine. I said hastily that I had not yet received instructions from my government, and I left him. This time I determined to get rid of him for good, and had my breakfast brought to my room, explaining to him when we met that I was holding early-morning conferences and would no longer go down to the breakfast room.

But in looking back over the points he had brought up in our conversations I realized I had been permitted an advance glimpse of the long-range Russian objective.

I warned my Filipino fellow delegates: "Be careful of that young man. Beyond doubt he has been assigned to our delegation to try to win us to Russia's side."

Directly after I showed my coldness to the young Russian I spoke in session at the United Nations. As I sat down, Molotov demanded the floor. Pointing at me, he demanded bitterly: "What is the Philippine delegate doing here? And the delegate from India? These two countries are not independent and they should not be here."

From that hour on we were adversaries.

That did not prevent him from inviting me to his parties, which were the most splendid given in the United Nations. Never have I seen such luxury as was displayed at the first party given by Molotov in the St. Francis Hotel. The entire conference was crowded into the largest ballroom, where tables were covered with the most costly delicacies, and I was particularly impressed by an enormous flag in colored caviar. The hammer-and-sickle was made of red caviar; it was an object of mouth-watering beauty.

Molotov proved to be the most affable of hosts. Urbane, bland, well-mannered, he moved about with a word for everyone. What a change from the juggernaut of the sessions!

As the conference wore on I noticed that Molotov gave private dinners to each of the delegations in turn, and that he scrupulously attended the parties given by all the other delegates. Also, whenever a chief delegate spoke, Molotov was the first to reach his side with congratulations.

Those who say the Russians are not diplomats are wrong. They know where it is effective to show courtesy and when it will make a sounder impression to behave like gangsters.

Their lavish entertaining in San Francisco brought to mind a memory of a Rotary Convention I had attended in Cleveland long before the war. At that convention everyone yielded before the delegate from Japan, who was both friendly and firm in purpose, and who had arrived with two large trunks filled with the most exquisite gifts—fans, kimonos, fancy shirts—for the United States delegates.

These he had dealt out to the United States delegates with a lavish hand, and that night he had come to my room and his first words to me in private were a contemptuous attack on the United States.

The Russians were playing the same game. They drew the spotlight on themselves and flattered the American delegates with lavish affairs. In private they never missed an opportunity to belittle America. Their attempts to poison minds showed them to be no friends of the United States.

I parried their insults against America too many times. After a time they gave me up as hopeless.

But they were royally entertained in San Francisco. They were shown everything. Docks, shipyards, industries of every kind—all were opened up before the Soviets.

I told my friends Charles Wheeler, former president of Rotary International, and Fred Stevenot, once president of the Bank of America: "Why are the important places of defense being shown to the Russians? Look out for them. They are going to be your worst enemies."

But the best parties given in San Francisco in those days of the founding of the United Nations were given in honor of the delegates from Russia.

Again, I warned the members of my own delegation: "These Russians are not here for a peace conference. They are here to perfect and promote their blueprint of conquest. Watch between their words for the outline of that blueprint. It will be similar to the one followed by Japan."

I would be proven right. In every country Russia has attacked, she has followed the pattern attempted by the

36

Rising Sun. I left San Francisco firmly convinced that sooner or later there would be a rift between the Soviet Union and the United States.

My admiration for Russia was gone. It had been replaced by the darkest suspicions. What I had seen and heard in San Francisco had made me positive that while the plan of the Rising Sun had failed, Russia had taken it over, determined this time to make it work. It was clearly a global plan to be put into effect all at once on many fronts.

The attack was launched before we knew.

We attained our independence the year after the founding of the United Nations, and shortly after I again took temporary leave of my duties in the United Nations and returned to the Philippines at the request of President Roxas to campaign for the approval of the Philippine Trade Act, which was to be voted on in a national plebiscite.

This is the Bell Act, the law governing economic relations between the United States and the Philippines. It sets increasing tariffs on mutual exchange of raw materials from the Philippines and manufactured goods from the United States, from 1954 to 1974, when full tariffs are supposed to apply. Such a measure could be enforced only after its approval by the Filipino people in a plebiscite.

Roxas wanted me to go about the country with him and help explain the Trade Act to our people and ask them to support it. It was during this tour of my homeland that I learned that Communism in the Philippines no longer consisted of a few submerged and scattered cells sending up bubbles here and there in the national consciousness. Within the brief time I had been away, Communism had not only made a bold appearance in our Christian republic. It was definitely on the rise.

Chapter III

ROXAS as President had proved to be all we had hoped for: an honest and able executive with a fine grasp of the moral and economic problems facing the Philippines. He had accomplished so much in so short a time, and won the loyalty of such a large percentage of the people, that one found it hard to believe a secret cancer had begun to nibble at the heart of the Philippines.

All Roxas had accomplished or was trying to do met with opposition from the new force rising in the land—the Communists.

Now they were attacking the Philippine Trade Act. It was not perfect, we knew, but it was the best we could get at the time, and Roxas felt the people might understand it better if I campaigned to explain its workings.

Traveling over the Philippines making speeches, I found the people were buoyant and confident, and praise of Roxas was heard everywhere. And still, carping voices were heard. Roxas and his splendid supporters worked under a running fire of disapproval. The Trade Act had come under the fire of the Communists; they had served, then, to bring me home.

Right away, I shared the barrage of Red hatred. It

seemed that the worst they could say of me was that I was pro-American. All sorts of charges were made against me, some of them strange indeed to a man who had worked all his life with one purpose always in mind: the freeing of his country.

Now we had that freedom, and I was being vilified for being grateful to the great friendly nation that had voluntarily set us free!

In the United Nations I had argued against the Communists. Now I was actually fighting them for the first time in my own country. It seemed inconceivable that they had been able to take so firm and secret a grasp on the Philippines, and in so brief a time.

As I have said, there had been a few red bubbles rising here and there to the surface, even before the war. One group in the province of Pampanga had even succeeded in electing a Communist mayor (who, by the way, had been educated in the United States and at one time was employed in the post office in Chicago).

We must not forget the significant fact that this movement began in and was limited then to Pampanga, a province of huge land holdings, where the tenant farmers were so mistreated by some of their wealthy absentee landlords that many were still paying off the debts of their great-great-grandfathers, increased by the centuries, which they could never hope to pay off in their lifetime but must pass on to enslave their sons.

The leader of these pioneer subversives was one Pedro Abad Santos, who started as a convinced Socialist.

When the war broke out these men became guerrillas

40

and fought heroically and long against the Japanese. During the war Pedro Abad Santos died.

After the war a new crop of leaders rose in their ranks. One was outstanding—the labor leader Crisanto Evangelista, a printer by trade who had organized the Printers' Union in the Philippines. He had visited Moscow and been indoctrinated there with Communism. Another was the fiery Luis Taruc, no longer a student organizing "literary parties."

As soon as the war ended and the elections were held, Luis Taruc entered the arena as a full-fledged politician under the hammer-and-sickle. He was the only Communist candidate to win a seat in our Lower House.

Communism had been outlawed as seditious in the Philippines while Manuel L. Quezon was still President of the Commonwealth. Acting on the fact that Communism was an outlaw party, the house members voted to deprive Taruc of his seat. Thus ousted, Taruc made no more efforts to fight in the open. He left Manila and fled to the hills. There he joined the guerrillas, who were already causing disorder in the province. He was joined, in his self-imposed exile, by his friend and advisor, the former university professor, Dr. Vicente Lava.

Now they were organizing the bands of guerrillas into a Red Army of the Philippines. These were the Huks, and they were already laying their plans to take over a country struggling to rise above ruin.

The scope of their plans was not yet apparent. We could only see that there was trouble. There were sporadic outbursts and attempts to intimidate, and a great deal of scurrilous talk. There were also threats, and these became

41

louder as the campaign for the Trade Act went on and the approaching plebiscite promised victory for our side.

The night before the general vote was to be taken, a huge mass meeting was held in the Plaza Miranda in Manila. I believe about one hundred thousand people attended to hear the two speakers for the Trade Act—President Roxas and myself. I spoke first, then President Roxas made his speech and sat down, and just as I was shaking his hand to congratulate him a bomb exploded on the grandstand. The photographer standing before us to take our picture absorbed most of the bomb fragments; poor fellow, his life saved ours. Another man standing four feet away was killed.

In the confusion we saw a man running through the crowd. He was caught by police. We learned he was a Communist, a barber named Guillen. He had occupied a seat directly under the grandstand and from there he had tossed the bomb.

At the time the most important fact to us all was that Roxas had been saved.

About five o'clock the next morning a weeping woman knocked at the door of my room in the Manila Hotel. I recognized her as the wife of Amado V. Hernandez, a brilliant young poet, writer, and orator, in the vernacular, who before the war had edited the Tagalog language newspaper *Mabuhay*. He had been a regular attendant at the "literary parties" and had given several in his own home.

He was a man I liked very much and in whom I had implicit faith. After the war, when I had no newspaper work for him—in fact no newspaper—he had asked me to recommend him to a position with the U.S. Army in the Philippines. This I did gladly, and he was employed as a translator of Tagalog in Press Relations. Then while in the United States I had heard with surprise that he was no longer with the army, but was running for Councilman in Manila.

People began asking me if I had heard any of his speeches. "They're downright subversive," I was told. "The man must be a Communist."

Amado Hernandez was the last person I would have expected to fall for Kremlin propaganda, and I lost no opportunity to say so, to everyone who mentioned his name. So for the past year I had defended him, from my distant post in the United States.

Now his wife was at my door, weeping. The barber Guillen who had thrown the bomb at the rally had confessed he had been urged into the act by Amado Hernandez.

She told me that her husband had been arrested and that the fiscal, as we call the district attorney, had refused both men bail. She believed in his innocence, and she convinced me. Also, he was a former employee and fellow worker and I had trusted him implicitly for years.

So I telephoned the fiscal. He was not pleased at being roused so early. He was less pleased when he learned what I wanted. In fact, he sounded shocked.

"General, don't you know the man's a Communist?" he said.

I said I knew nothing of the sort. And I added, "I have just come from America where a man is held innocent until he is proven guilty. We have also been trained in that belief. I believe Hernandez is innocent, and I hope you will see your way clear to allow him to go out on bail."

Hernandez was set free. Guillen remained in jail. The case came to trial and Hernandez was acquitted. Guillen, the scapegoat for Moscow ideology, was executed.

I was to meet again with Hernandez.

Meantime, the plebiscite had come and gone, and the Trade Act had been approved by an overwhelming majority.

I returned to New York and the United Nations, pleased with the results of the campaign and with all that was being accomplished in the Philippines and thanking God that Roxas had been spared. In spite of all the postwar difficulties, he had assumed a normal leadership. He was restoring the government agencies, he had reopened the courts, and was rebuilding the roads and areas wrecked by the Japanese in their final orgy of murder and destruction. But beyond all, he had reunited a people who had been divided during the war between the collaborators and the pro-Americans. Of all the ugly tasks Roxas had to face, this had been the worst, built as it was on bitterness and suspicion.

In New York one of my pleasanter duties as permanent delegate to the United Nations was entertaining visitors from the Philippines. One day a surprising visitor arrived at our Philippine Mission offices. It was Hernandez, only now he had achieved another metamorphosis and was a labor leader. He told me that he had been sent to the United States to study its labor conditions and that his trip was being financed by the Filipino labor unions.

His had been an eventful journey from Manila. Evidently American Intelligence had reports concerning him, for in Honolulu he was detained for questioning by the immigration authorities. Directly after being released he called a press conference and gave out statements that made shocking headlines around the world. He charged that American immigration authorities had abused and humiliated him because he was a Filipino, and that there was no freedom to be found in the United States.

While I regretted this incident I could not understand it, and I did not learn until later that he proceeded to San Francisco and had a visit with Harry Bridges, the labor leader long accused of Communist affiliations.

I received him in New York as I would any visitor from home: took him to the sessions, was photographed with him, and autographed the photograph as a souvenir of his visit.

He did not leave New York.

It seemed that everywhere one turned, there was Hernandez, and always as the inseparable companion of a temporary member of our Philippine Mission to the United Nations. I had chosen this young fellow out of many university students in Manila for his potentialities of leadership, his intelligence, his liberal views and fine appearance. He was one of the brightest of our young men. He gave every promise of a brilliant career in the service of our country, and I had determined to help him as much as was in my power.

Let us call him Roberto.

Apparently, these two met in New York as strangers. When I learned that they lived at the same hotel, I thought that since both were strangers in a new land, it was natural that they should become companions.

When a man has four sons of his own he likes to think of himself as understanding of youth. Whenever Roberto came into our office to ask for one of his temporary assignments—he was not a regular member of my staff—he always carried a copy of the *Daily Worker*. I decided he had a right to read at first hand the writings of the leftists if only to know how to argue against them. Of his frequently voiced anti-religious views I thought leniently: He is young!

(Alger Hiss was also young. So young, and so unassuming, that I gave him no importance during the founding of the United Nations. I do not remember Hiss as having played a conspicuous role at San Francisco.)

As time went on I placed additional semiofficial responsibilities on Roberto. He became my trusted aide. Life in the United Nations can be hectic. With six committees meeting all at once no single individual can attend to all. I often sent representatives from the Philippine Mission to vote according to my instructions, and Roberto with his swift and easy way of summing up situations became my favorite messenger to carry these instructions.

Several incidents displeased me, but he could explain them away. Once he told me he planned to attend a controversial political meeting. I told him that the members or friends of members of a diplomatic corps are not supposed to attend the partisan political affairs of another country. He seemed to agree with me. Later I learned he had been at the meeting.

Again, I thought: He is young.

46

I gave him more responsibilities as the need arose.

Then came sessions in Europe—Rome, London, Geneva, and Paris. Roberto was indispensable over there. Also who should be with us, hovering around the Assembly in Paris, but Hernandez! He seemed to have forgotten all about his assignment to study labor conditions in the United States. Here he was as an unrecognized attendant to the United Nations, living in the same hotel with Roberto, and being seen with him everywhere.

As long as Roberto's work did not suffer it seemed none of my business. It was pleasant that the boy had a friend from his own country on this side of the world.

While we were in Paris a case came up in the General Assembly. Jan Papanek of Czechoslovakia, who had become *persona non grata* with the Communists in his own country and had taken political refuge in the United States, was a candidate for the Administrative Board. He had served on the Board before, and as I knew him personally and admired him for his ability, I pledged myself to Papanek and instructed Roberto to tell the member who was to represent me in the committee that he was to vote for Papanek. My instructions were specific.

Several days later, chatting in a group in the lobby, I expressed myself as sorry that Papanek had not been elected. Someone said bitterly, "Why are you sorry, since you did not vote for him?" I was indignant. "Certainly I voted for Papanek! I gave specific instructions . . ."

Roberto took my scolding with his usual calm. "I misunderstood you."

He could not have misunderstood. I can see that now,

and much else. At the time I felt that I had unwittingly double-crossed a fine man black-listed by the Soviets.

This was particularly annoying to me, since by this time I had foisted upon me in the General Assembly the role of principal antagonist of the Communist delegates. I knew that in the Papanek matter I had lost out to the Communists, and I blamed my own stupidity in failing to make myself understood. It did not occur to me to blame Roberto, who was so willing and intelligent, and so young.

Some time after this, he decided to return to Manila. I gladly assisted him to a responsible post and I said good-bye to him with perfect faith in his integrity and his chances for advancement. With him, back to Manila, went his inseparable companion, Hernandez.

I shall say no more of Hernandez. He will not figure again in this account of what was taking place in the Philippines, beyond the fact that at present he is in prison, serving time for sedition. But I am only trying to show how segments that at the time seemed very small and unimportant were being cleverly fitted together until there appeared all at once before our unbelieving eyes the completed pattern. Under our very noses, too close for us to see, was the pattern Moscow was pushing together with such devilish exactitude in the Philippines.

Certainly we did not suspect the place in the pattern reserved for the so-young and so-willing Roberto. Every report from the Philippines told of the good work he was doing in Manila.

But while I remained unaware of what was being worked out in my own country, the role of Russia in the United Nations had become only too clear. The organization of the Freedom of Information Conference under the auspices of the United Nations in Geneva in 1948 brought out new and surprising facets of the Soviet character.

It was there Russia showed her true colors for the first time, not only to the conference, but to the world.

At Geneva we saw the Russians not as the surly boors of the United Nations, but as suave masters of diplomacy. Sixty-four nations were represented, including some, such as Albania, Austria, and Switzerland, which were not members of the United Nations. Despite the great size of the gathering it was in this conference that we succeeded in getting unanimous votes, and for the surprising reason that the famed Russian *"Niet"* was conspicuous by its absence. This I believe was because Ambassador Alexander Bogomolov, the chief Soviet delegate and one of their ablest diplomats, wanted to convince the world that Russians did not always take the contrary stand; that they could be amiable and reasonable.

But it soon became apparent that this amiability and reasonableness was reserved for matters non-essential to foreign policy, and that in all matters pertaining to the United States they were adamant as ever. Their iron purpose was veiled under a show of courtesy, but it was there. Bogomolov knew all the old tricks of the magician and the defense attorney and the diplomat, of making important issues seem unimportant and trivial issues appear of overwhelming importance. In lobby or salon or bar the Russians were relaxed and friendly, but once on the floor or in the chair and an issue arose that really mattered—then they were fanatics. It was as if a signal were given and masks donned again.

A great deal of Bogomolov's success at Geneva, socially and otherwise, was due to his charming wife, who spoke English well and acted as his secretary and interpreter and hostess. She was as intelligent as she was attractive and was, of all things, a civil engineer! She had made many friends for Russia before the conference at Geneva ended.

So while in the United Nations we had been repelled by the arrogance and aloofness of the Russian delegates, in Geneva we were struck by their friendliness. They were leaning backwards to be friendly and make friends, and on every hand delegates of other nations could be heard remarking, "Say, the Russians aren't such bad fellows! Not stubborn at all, once you get to know them!"

My own suspicions, roused at San Francisco, were slow to die. I cannot believe in these national overnight sea changes. Has the soul of Nazi Germany been changed? Or the ancient spirit of Japan?

So at Geneva, amidst all the smiling and bowing and handshaking, I still found myself wondering, is this actually the new Russia? Can we believe in this expansive mood?

Every minute of their waking hours the Russians were at work winning friends. I noticed as the days went on that they were not only winning friends for their side, they were winning friends *away from the West*. This was an unmistakable peace offensive they were conducting in the guise of congeniality and conviviality.

Their campaign had one curious result. Heretofore in international conferences the Great Powers had paid little

50

attention to the small nations. In this, the Western world had erred.

In San Francisco for the first time the small nations had been given consideration and the right to speak, and for this, and for only this, we can thank the Soviet.

One of the most revered members of the United Nations, respected even by Molotov and Vishinsky, was Joseph Bech, a truly great leader who was chairman of the delegation from Luxembourg. He told us how he had represented Luxembourg as its Prime Minister at the Treaty of Versailles, and in the presence of Wilson and Clemenceau was pleading the cause of his small country, when a representative of one of the larger powers asked: "Where is this country of yours? I can't see it on the map."

And Bech had answered smartly: "Of course you can't see it, because it is under your thumb."

I know how he felt, because when the design for the United Nations emblem was drawn at Lake Success, the world map centering the design did not show the Philippines at all. I protested, and the designer protested back.

"If we put the Philippines on, it will show no bigger than a pinpoint," he argued.

I said, "Put the pinpoint there."

And it is there, and you see it only if you look with care, but the fact that we are on the map means a great deal to our small nation.

No matter how small the country, it not only has its rights, but may have great importance; how and when, no one can foresee. The lad with his finger in the dike was only a very small boy, but according to the legend, he saved his country from inundation. That can be taken as a modern parable. Consider Greece after World War II, when so-called guerrillas from Albania and other puppet states infiltrated there, indoctrinated the citizens with Communism and succeeded in turning Greek against Greek. Greece was rapidly changing into another puppet state.

Russia's main objective there was one that had always been denied Russia—to go through Greece and use it as their outlet into the Mediterranean. This Soviet plan would have snipped Europe in two and denied the Western powers the right to the Suez Canal. It would have turned Europe over to the Soviet.

America stopped that plan. General James Van Fleet was sent there with American military strategists to help train the Greek patriots, who held their little land against the Soviets.

Eight million resisting Greeks prevented the carrying out of this plan even as they had prevented during the Second World War the planned meeting of Hitler's and Mussolini's troops in their country. Greece by its delaying action made it possible for Eisenhower to land in Africa and later in Anzio.

In the Philippines, the delaying action of four precious months in Bataan and Corregidor gave Australia and the Pacific Coast time to prepare; this according to the statement of Chief of Staff Marshall.

These are two small countries that played important roles in the democratic defense in World War II.

The United States, England, and France, conscious of their own powers, had always before ignored the opinions of the tinier nations. Here were the Russians, deferring to us and paying us the attention that had never before been ours, and this, by contrast, did us a great deal of good. It was beyond the realization of many of the delegates of the previously ignored countries that this good was being done out of the hatred Russia bore the great Western powers, and Russia's determination to belittle the United States, England, and France.

Even though the Russians were by this time well aware of my pronounced antagonism, they still tried to win me because I belonged with the smaller nations. When I was fighting for Philippine reparations in the Far Eastern Commission in Washington and was obliged to make statements not too favorable to America, the Russian delegates always paid me congratulatory visits later to commend my statements; the effect was always that I made a point of softening my comments at the next session.

At Geneva I was nominated for the presidency of the Freedom of Information Conference, whereupon the Russians immediately backed another man, the delegate from India. They must have felt I was a strong candidate, because the day before the election one of their delegates came to tell me in emphatic terms that they would support me. I had been so certain they were against me that I doubted this pledge, so after the election, I asked to have the votes counted. I knew every country that had been pledged to me, and by the count I was able to tell that I had definitely not received the Russian vote.

However, the offer had been made in the friendliest fashion, and everything the Russians did at Geneva was done with every appearance of courtesy and charm.

As before, I was invited to their parties and to the affairs given by their satellites, where the customary Soviet propaganda was passed around with the boundless supply of liquor and the excellent Russian foods. Pamphlets were handed out, or motion pictures shown, displaying all that was being accomplished under Soviet rule in Poland or Czechoslovakia or some other puppet land, and everything they did was well done.

It seemed to me they were always giving parties or attending parties. Our dour Russians had become the playboys of the conference. They were everywhere; they mixed with everyone.

I noticed also in Geneva that as a rule the American delegates spent much of their time together. Evenings, in restaurants, they would be seen dining together, a tight band of compatriots in a foreign land. At the time it struck me that they would learn more and give a better impression if they mixed more with the other nationalities, as the Russians were doing.

One evening in Geneva a dinner was given in my honor by the delegate of Lebanon. I happened to glance toward the door and saw my aide, Major Cesar B. Jimenez, and my son Gregorio standing there. By the expression of shock on their faces I knew something terrible had happened. They hurried to me, and one whispered, "We have had a phone call from Washington." My first thought was of my wife, then one of them whispered, "President Roxas has just died."

I had to excuse myself to my hosts and withdraw, trembling with an emotion composed of both relief, since Virginia was safe, and utter despair.

Once again, and in a time of dreadful need, the Philippines was left leaderless. We had had a great leader in Quezon. He died in the critical time when we were trying to recapture the Philippines. Now, only two years after we had become independent and made Roxas our President, he was dead. Elpidio Quirino, Vice President, took the oath of office.

The death of Manuel Roxas was symbolic. He was speaking at Clark Field, an American Army air base in the Philippines. He completed his speech with the dramatic promise that the Philippines was ready to throw all its forces behind America in the fight against Communism. Just as he finished making this pledge, he collapsed.

He was picked up by American doctors and carried to an American hospital on the field. There he died, on American soil in the Philippines.

In this most critical time in our country's history, we had lost our greatest leader. What followed was inevitable —graft, corruption, and the resultant scandals that ruin the faith of a people.

Chapter IV

ELPIDIO QUIRINO'S administration was to last six
years and it would be blamed for many of the ills that almost ended democracy in the Philippines. This is unjust.
No single individual can be blamed for all that happened
to us in the postwar period which we had hoped would
be dedicated to peace and rebuilding.

He became President when Roxas died, on April 15,
1948. Within a few months our fledgling republic was
riven with scandals and hatreds that threatened our very
lives, while the world watched with bewilderment and
horror, and even the Filipinos themselves failed to understand how this debacle had been brought about and what
was being done to them.

Quirino had fallen heir to evils centuries old.

The effects of moral disintegration had been manifest
when President Sergio Osmeña returned to the liberated
Philippines in 1944 and hopefully assumed leadership over
a people who had been forced by three-and-a-half years
of war and resistance into ways antithetical to four hundred years of Christian education and forty years of training in democracy.

The wise guidance of Osmeña and the firm wisdom of

Roxas had served temporarily to quell the danger and promise a resumption of normalcy. But the dignified Osmeña had not chosen to campaign when his time came up for election, and as a result, Roxas was elected. When Roxas died, Quirino came to power. Quirino proved helpless as situation after situation arose that needed stamping out there and then, and thus these dangers were permitted to spread and create greater evil.

Only a few months after Quirino took office the tides of democracy, which had been rising so gloriously in our islands, turned and began ebbing in the opposite direction.

To understand the danger we must look at the Philippines not as a small segment of democracy in the Far East, but as a part of that vast, mysterious, and ancient continent of Asia.

Asia had been in a state of revolution for centuries.

From the beginning of this century up to the shock attack at Pearl Harbor, the larger part of this vast continent was changing from a picturesque legendary area of silken-clad rajas and geishas, elephants and cherry blossoms, into a seething cauldron of revolt that covered half the world.

The spirit of revolution stemmed from the common root of the basic human urge for release from alien domination. Let us admit at once that in the case of Asia this meant freedom from the domination of the European, which is to say the White Man. This urge had been voiced in Asia in many ways, mostly in acts of violence. The Taiping rebellion in China, the Sepoy mutiny in India, the succeeding waves of minor revolts and uprisings all over the mainland, and, not the least in the preceding century, the Filipino's successful revolt against Spain, all these had been protests against the domination of the alien White.

So the beginning of the twentieth century found Asia boiling with resentment, but the might of European superiority in weapons held down the cover, and acts of protest were in the main confined to sporadic outbursts of violence. The strength of the movement grew with a wider diffusion of the ideals and ideas of liberation, and the growing passion for release.

For the next forty years that passion swelled to the breaking point; revolution in Asia became no longer a series of isolated outbreaks, but a vast, widespread, and inexorable human movement. The Boxer uprising was a foreshadowing of events to come, which for the first time imposed its bitter truths on all the Western world, not only on a single imperial power. The Russo-Japanese war of 1904-1905 proved to the Asian that he could meet and defeat the European, and that by the simple expedient of making himself proficient in the use of the European's arms. It is no accident that the demand for freedom, which has been called the nationalist upsurge of Asia, gained momentum in the years following the Russo-Japanese war.

These forty years saw the complete fruition of that dream. Gandhi carried a Christlike doctrine to India's millions that resulted in the "revolution of love." In Indonesia's great Isles of Spice, Sukarno, Sjahrir, and Hatta preached to the millions the rebirth of a new Sri-Visayan empire built on the broadest basis of freedom and equality. China's starveling hordes were aroused by Sun Yat-sen

58

to a new awareness of their rights as human beings. While in Japan, ruthless and ambitious leaders were harnessing a new and terrible machine, the technology of the West, to the greed of an empire-minded and conquest-inspired people.

All these either aimed directly at the elimination of the White Man as the ruler of Asia, or, like Sun, built upon the natural and legitimate urge for freedom the foundations for a new economic order, which in the end proved to be no order, and scarcely economic.

The result, in the vast hinterland of Asia, was the transformation of a great reservoir of mankind—one billion human beings—from the legendary area of mystery, philosophy, and glamour into a seething mass of newly aware and grimly struggling humanity, aware from its top through its lowest levels of powerful new forces which were speedily dissolving the ancient creed of man's superiority to man.

Here then, in Asia, was a positive trend toward a Western democracy which the nations of the West either ignored or were meeting in differing ways. The colonial powers of Europe wavered between open resistance and a policy of inertia, some chancellories apparently waiting for the hypothetical meeting of irresistible force with immovable body.

The trend was given impetus by new ideals of the social relationships imported from the West; by improvements of communications and transportation; by the acquisition and knowledge of the White Man's weapons; by the assimilation on the part of the Eastern peoples of the technological sciences of the West; by the defeat of White Russia at the hands of the Japanese; and, not least of all, by the democratic example set during these forty years by America in the Philippines.

Out of this change a new and menacing force leveled against white supremacy began spreading between the Urals and the Pacific. While European powers hesitated before it, or staged demonstrations of violence that in turn bred violence, America met the force head-on in the Philippine Commonwealth in characteristic American fashion, and conquered it there, not with counterforce, not with the paternalistic assumption of the "white man's burden," but with a cooperative way of living in which the burdens and rewards were shared with all the people, and where freedom and responsibility were synonymous terms.

During the first part of this century democracy in its purest form was being fostered in the Philippines, and the burdens of state and of economy were shared there by devoted Americans and devoted Filipinos.

Technically, the Philippines became a possession of the United States in 1900 and retained that status until 1935, when by the operation of the Tydings-McDuffie Act it became the Philippine Commonwealth, with Manuel Quezon as first President and with increased autonomous powers. This status was to be held for ten years, or until 1945, when the basic condition of a "stable government" as outlined in the Jones Act of 1916 would be fully attained, and full independence proclaimed.

So in 1900, before the Russo-Japanese war and in no way influenced by it, the United States of America, finding itself with an Asian possession on its hands for the first time, had ignored the examples of the imperialistic, colonizing European countries in Asia and begun its own novel program for democracy in the Philippines.

The crusade was composed of two complementary parts. The basis was political self-rule. The second part, that of political and economic preparation, was to serve as safeguard against the dangers of immaturity when independence came.

This was total rejection of the European approach to the Asian as "the white man's burden." The American attitude from the beginning was that the "burden"—which was to be admitted—was a responsibility to be shared, and that the relationship between East and West was not and could never be that of master and slave, but was based on the duty of power in being to extend its strength to power latent.

Its roots were in the American declaration of the equality of man before his Creator and of his endowment in the eyes of all other men with the "inalienable rights." Stemming from these roots was the concept that it is the inescapable duty of the stronger man to assist his weaker equal before God in establishing and maintaining those rights.

For the next forty years, in successive stages, America maintained unbroken its course in assisting the Filipino people to attain democracy in its most comprehensive sense, carrying out to the full the pledge made by President Woodrow Wilson, "no backward step shall be taken." Politically and economically (more rapidly in the former field it is true) the Filipinos were progressing toward complete sovereignty; they had almost attained their goal.

While this lesson of democracy was being taught in the

Philippines, while America was gradually strengthening the Philippines against the day it would release its last hold on our Islands and wish us well in our great adventure in freedom, elsewhere in Asia the ruling powers still clung to the vestiges of their domination.

Their attention was diverted toward Europe by World War II.

Then Japan rose on the crest of the great revolutionary wave moving over Asia—Japan, the little country that by defying and defeating great White Russia back in 1904 had been the first to show Asia that the White Man was not Superman; that he too could be made to suffer imprisonment and shame, to shed tears, suffer, and die.

Japan now, temporarily, rose to hideous power.

In World War II Japan confirmed the findings of the Russo-Japanese war, holding the mightiest Western nations in the shadow of Pacific defeat for more than three years.

The sneak attack on Pearl Harbor was followed by the conquest of the Philippines, then by the three-and-a-half years of Japanese occupation. Americans and Filipinos who had fought together now suffered together, but this was no supine yielding to superior forces. The Filipino resistance movement is accorded in history a place no lower than those allotted to France, Belgium, and Poland. In our Islands, as in those European countries, the "underground" was not confined to a few die-hard resistants. It was national. It affected all strata of the population. The very children took part in the fight that seemed unending, that inevitably brought with it a transformation in values that temporarily made wrong seem right, and black, if not white, at least appear to be a very light shade of gray.

Then America rallied to the liberation of the captive Philippines and there followed months of devastating fighting within the land, and the equally devastating retreat by the Japanese as they were pushed back into the sea, burning, raping, looting, killing, laying waste the areas of their retreat with a hatred doubled in intensity because we, the Asian Filipinos, had fought against the Japanese who were also Asian.

Conquest, resistance, and victory—these filled the years wherein the Filipinos knew little except terror, suffering, and deprivation in every form. Small wonder that when freedom came we as a people were ill prepared for the newer and more incomprehensible problems that were to come with victory.

On August 15, 1945, the Japanese emperor formally announced to his people that in the interests of peace he would act to end the conflict, which, as Hiroshima and Nagasaki and the combined invading spearheads of MacArthur, Nimitz, and Halsey made plain, was almost over. The power which had threatened to engulf all Asia, with undercurrents of a subsequent bid for world empire, lay prostrate.

Not only Japan was supine, but all Asia lay prostrate in the aftermath of war. The whole region was in ruins, and only the spirit of revolt burned on with small, flickering flames in a vast area of devastation.

And Japan, the loser—what did defeat mean to Japan?

In the three-and-a-half years between Pearl Harbor and Hiroshima the Japanese had succeeded in removing from other Asian minds any lingering doubts there may have been of the Asian's capacity to meet and overcome his erstwhile European overlords. Japan almost won the war, and she won what victories she had under a powerful slogan: "Asia for the Asians."

But Japan prostituted the leadership which she nearly achieved by inordinate greed. Her slogan was only superficially "Asia for the Asians." In effect and in substance, the propaganda trumpets of the Hoo Doo Bu had blared out the gospel of "Asia for the Japanese." She had wooed us all, from the Philippines to the Urals, with the flattering refrain, "We are your fellow Asians. Join us in driving the White Man into the sea!"

Asia, freedom-loving, quick to recognize the new threat of overlordship in another form, had repelled the advance of Japan and joined with the West to destroy her.

During that period of war the Asian learned his own strength. Over the tramping of Japanese army boots there had been heard a consistent deeper cry of "Asia for the Asians." Asia spoke with one voice, as long as Asians faced the common danger. For a time they had but one objective, the overthrow of an arrogant aggressor.

When Japan collapsed, the unity of Asia began to fall apart, lacking as it did the cement of a common threat. In the place of that unity there began a diversity of regional aspirations, but in one sense they still shared the same objective, which was, as before, freedom from alien rule.

So the Asian's centuries-old determination to be free of foreign domination was strengthened by war and the defeat of Japan. With the aggressor Japan out of the way, surely the White Man could be forced out of the Far East, even by a weakened and depleted Asia!

This became the postwar Oriental dream.

There was one country in the Orient that had no part in this dream. In the ruined Philippines, one year after Japan surrendered, we saw the birth of the Philippine Republic. Behind us lay three-and-a-half years of social and moral devastation. Ahead lay years of struggle and economic insecurity. But the enlightened policy of the United States was carrying through the planned transition of a dependent people to national sovereignty and full independence, an independence, furthermore, the security of which was to be insured by a continuing policy of economic cooperation. Our freedom had been achieved in a spirit of full understanding and mutual cooperation.

Therefore, we had no quarrel with the White Man in the Philippines. Physically, economically, and spiritually, our losses were beyond calculation, but the future was on our side. Our victory in the war was a moral one, we had sided with democracy and democracy was the winner. America was our co-partner and friend.

In other parts of Asia the transition to freedom was not so peacefully achieved. From the Arabian Sea to the Straits of Sunda freedom would be obtained only after bitter struggles, around the conference tables and even in the open fields of war.

So we must realize that while Japan lost in its blueprint of war, it was the winner in its attack against the White Man in Asia. Long after the Emperor gave his dignified signal of withdrawal, the fight against white domination went on in other parts of Asia.

The fighting did not stop in Indonesia, where a reluctant Netherlands refused to give up her richest possession.

In Indochina the war-born passion to end alien rule turned the people there against the French. Throughout the entire mainland of southeast Asia the fires lighted by the Rising Sun burned on and the fight for freedom continued to rage in lands ravaged by war, with their communications and age-old social orders in ruins, with all the old values lost, and all passion spent save the indestructible urge for release from alien rule. Which, in Asia, means "against white supremacy."

Then into these leaderless and chaotic areas of desolation, hunger, and death, a newer and louder voice took up the cry of: "Asia for the Asians." It came out of Moscow and it threatened to shake the world.

To the underprivileged man of Asia who had never known what it meant to go to bed with a full belly, Communism promised food and the right not to be bound to foreign rulers—a will-o'-the-wisp Paradise to be won only by yielding the freedom he did not possess to a Soviet scheme for world conquest. He did not know that Russia planned to conquer his side of the world. Ideology meant nothing to the common man of Asia, who in fact had for countless centuries possessed a far better ideology of ethics and morals than anything that had originated in Moscow. He knew only that his stomach had hunger, that his wife lay dead of hunger, that his children died covered with sores and eaten by flies because he had no food to give them. He knew that for him there was work without sufficient returns to maintain life, an existence without hope; cruelties, indignities, and debasement, and never a chance of Justice.

For these he blamed the White Man.

To such starvelings the preachings of Marx were without meaning. All that mattered was a fistful of rice, a bowl of tea, the right to live. Give that ragged skeleton a gun and tell him, "Fight! Fight for your country and its foreign overlords!" and what would he answer?

Why should he fight for white men!

But he would fight for a change. Any change.

That is the litany of those who have lost faith in the governments of the lands they live in. "Any change is better than this."

This was the cry in China. In Indonesia. In Indochina.

This was the cry of the starving and it was not heard in London, Paris, the Hague. But it was heard in Moscow.

Moscow offered guns, and fed hatred. It does not matter to the oppressed whether the heel that holds it down is white or brown. It will be hated. The heel of the hated autocrat was on China, Indonesia, and Indochina, and to the haters Communism offered guns and the pledge that was lip service only: "Here is your chance at equality, our fellow Orientals. Here is your chance to drive out the White Man and be free and equal and well fed and self-respecting, like other men. . . ."

No, Communism did not express the longings of Asia. It served only to fill a vacuum. The leaders of the teeming millions of the Far East knew only one purpose—to drive the White Man out of Asia. On this, the Communists built their schemes for infiltration. They gave guns and advice to those who had lost faith. They gave them the cry:

"Asia for the Asians!"

With the same cry, Japan had launched her blueprint

of aggression, and had been halted only when she reached the Philippines.

Now Moscow was launching the same world-wide blueprint on the same cry, and once more, following Japan's example, the Russian campaign was headed straight for the Philippines.

By 1948 that campaign was well launched in every part of the world. The hate slogan of "Asia for the Asians" was not only being shouted in the ears of the Orientals, but in the United Nations it was being carefully voiced over cocktails and vodka and cups of steaming Russian tea. This was the year Roxas died and trouble really started in the Philippines; and in the General Assembly in Paris, where we went in session after Geneva, the Russian delegates were bold in letting their demands be known, not to their fellow delegates alone, but to all the listening world.

In Paris, in the Palais de Chaillot that September, with the shadow of war all over the world because of the Berlin blockade, the world saw how arrogant the new Russia could be. Here was none of the sweetness and light that had made notable the session at Geneva. Here for the first time we saw the belligerent Vishinsky and found him all out for aggression. Here was my first encounter with Vishinsky, and I may say we met head-on.

Vishinsky proved to be a dialectician and undefeatable in debate. Master of sophism, and of cynicism, he knew every trick and could twist any argument his way. In all his debates with me he showed a particular arrogance; it was plain that he had me pigeon-holed with the capitalists.

When I was elected chairman of the Ad Hoc Political and Security Committee, a committee that brought out the duplicity of the Russians as never before, I was appalled as agreements were made only to be disavowed the next day as if they had never been.

On the night before my committee was to vote on the admission of Ceylon to membership, one Polish-Soviet member of the committee actually signed an agreement with us and on the following day voted against us. Upon being shown the paper in the presence of witnesses he blandly denied ever having signed it. We were helpless.

How could we hold our own against such people? Religion, which exercises restraint in others, was lacking in the Russians and their satellites. Their religion was a fanatical creed set in Moscow, and no amount of reason nor appeals to decency could change them. They were unbending iron men, merciless as Nazis; they believed in their Moscow-set policies, and they were out to convince or kill.

In Paris for the first time I became certain that the Russians were inimical to world peace and that it was impossible for any of us among the democracies to come to terms with them.

All we could hope to do in the United Nations was to play a delaying game and try to keep murder out of the world a little while longer, with the hope that the miracle of peace might eventually be achieved.

In the year after this I became President of the General Assembly, and the afternoon of my inauguration Vishinsky held a press conference to announce that Russia had broken the monopoly of the atom bomb.

This terrifying bit of news was given out with deliberate intent, to show that the United States had better understand that Russia was not to be bulldozed by threats of the atom bomb, because she had it too!

The newsmen came to me to report this shocking news and I could only think back to my first impressions in San Francisco, when I had first suspected that Russia was the enemy of freedom and democracy. Now I knew that my first impressions had been right. It was after this that I turned all my efforts to help bring the Big Five together to an understanding and control of the atom bomb.

But as always, in private, the Russian delegates continued to exercise dignity and charm. At private affairs Vishinsky displayed manners worthy of a Russian aristocrat of the days of the Czars.

He liked to crack little jokes, and some were very witty. He paid compliments and made friends.

I recall one dinner I gave in New York for the Foreign Ministers attending the General Assembly sessions. Grover Whalen, who was then Chairman of the Mayor's Committee, offered a toast:

"To President and Mrs. Romulo, who have won the hearts of seven million New Yorkers."

Instantly, Vishinsky was on his feet with a glass upraised: "And to seven million New Yorkers, add one Russian!"

One night I invited him to the opera. *Manon Lescaut* was sung, and Vishinsky hummed every aria under his breath. It was easy to see that he loved music. He told me he played the violin.

His own social affairs were delightful and no expense was spared. I remember a dinner he gave at his headquarters on Park Avenue when Henri Spaak of Belgium and I were guests of honor. All the Russian and satellite delegates were there, about fourteen in all. Every effort was made by these charming people to please us, and still, no opportunity was missed to press home the Communist creed. These men were playing a desperate game and the rules were not to be forgotten for an instant. They created opportunities to get me alone to renew the subtle and by this time familiar approach:

"Since we are also Orientals . . ."

They were drumming that slogan on all the world fronts by this time. Hour after hour, on the far side of the Pacific, the Russian radio was sounding this formula in every Asian dialect into the listening ears of Asia: "We of Russia are your fellow Orientals. Join with us and drive out the hated White Man."

This was their propaganda cry in Paris and Geneva, Washington and New York, Tokyo, Manila, Shanghai. Russia was out to convince Asia that the colonial iniquities committed by the British, French, and Dutch were responsible for all the ills in the Far East, and that the Americans, because they also were white men, were no better than the hated colonial powers. But the Russians promised that once they were firmly linked to the Oriental peoples, they would treat them with the respect and consideration due their fellow Orientals. . . .

I could not take this propaganda seriously. I could not

71

imagine its being listened to with any respect in the Philippines. First, the Russians were not Orientals. These men were not like any Orientals I had ever known. The Russians do not think like Asians, or talk like them, or share their moral or religious creeds. And certainly they have nothing in common with the Filipinos, whose ancient culture is European, with a modern culture superimposed that came to us from America.

But to the frightened masses of Asia, who knew no difference between one race or another, who knew only white or brown, the Russian claim to kinship served to lull their suspicions of the Soviet and inflame their hatred against all whites. The Russian radio kept pounding this policy over the troubled Asian areas by night and by day in an insidious hate campaign calculated to turn Asia over to Russia and insure an easy Communist victory.

And because the Asian had learned hate and fear, he believed!

Behind the Russian argument was every scrawny native that was ever kicked by a booted white in the Orient; every twisted skeleton in rags that died of hunger before the doors of the white overlords; every native, no matter how intelligent or well-bred, who was refused entrance to a club or dining room in his own land; every sign that once stood in the public parks in Shanghai: "Chinese and dogs not allowed!"

Such incidents were thrown by Asia into the Communist balance.

All this was driving a wedge between the East and West and making understanding and friendship impossible between the two sides of the world. All this was being incorporated into the blueprint of Russia.

In Washington, as a representative on the Far Eastern Commission, I came into intimate contact for the first time with Russia's open truculence, arrogance, and insolence as shown toward all matters pertaining to America. This Commission had been set up amongst the nations that had fought Japan in order to help guide MacArthur in his task of democratizing the Japanese. In these meetings, called in the hope of achieving understanding, every statement concerning the United States brought forth words and expressions of utter contempt from the Russians. There were only eleven of us and we were in close contact, so I saw the Russian mind at very close range; Gromyko first, Malik next, then Panyushkin, and alternate delegates who were generals and admirals.

In San Francisco I had guessed at the dim outlines of the Communist blueprint. Now I saw it clearly outlined, and I knew my worst suspicions had been justified. Not only the United States, but all the Western powers were looked down upon by the Soviet state with arrogance and contempt.

It was clear that these people had but one aim—to submerge the United States.

That was all Russia needed. The other powers would collapse with America.

These arrogant and ruthless delegates filled me with a growing fear. They represented a country bent on world conquest.

On the other side of the world, their insidious and persistent campaign of hatred against the White Man was calculated to turn Asia over to Russia and insure an easy Communist victory in the Far East.

After that—as once planned in Berlin, and also in Tokyo —after that, the world!

So this was the Russian blueprint. Out in the open at last, and perfectly clear.

The hate-borne plan was far advanced by 1949. In the middle of that year, China, our neighbor and friend for many centuries, fell to the Communists.

Chapter V

THIS year of 1949 was the most critical in Philippine postwar history.

All the reports coming out of my country were of graft and corruption and of ugly flare-ups among the Filipinos themselves. In Geneva, Rome, Athens, New Delhi, Jakarta, New York, Washington, London, Rio de Janeiro, and Paris, I read these stories and felt sick at heart. Our little nation had just come into its own, and in this short time had become a byword. Everywhere I went I was questioned, jokingly or cynically, until even the friendliest queries became bitter to hear. Our shining hour had been turned into a nightmare.

How, and by whom? Had American teachings in the Philippines been wasted, or had we, the Filipinos, been unworthy of the responsibility of being a free people?

On what had become almost commuting trips across the world I studied the new problems in my country. There was no hiding the fact that the Philippines was in a bad way. The country was a powder keg, brimming with hatred, and at any moment it might explode.

I wondered about our new President. Was he powerful enough to keep the lid clamped down?

Quirino was a man of whom I had known very little, but he had been generous to me, retaining me in the position of Chief Delegate to the United Nations and giving me other and equally exacting posts as the months went by. I questioned friends who were wise in politics about him, and was answered with shrugged shoulders:

"Quirino? Oh, a fine man. But . . ."

And in the beginning the explanation would be given reluctantly: "Too many relatives has this man Quirino. And also, too many friends . . ."

The talk grew stronger. It became increasingly clear that while a few were getting very rich in the Philippines, the majority of the citizens were growing steadily poorer. The promised new roads, schools, buildings of every kind —where were they? While on the other hand, the newly rich were said to be standing very close to the walls of Malacañan, the historic palace in Manila where our presidents dwell.

Personally, I believe Quirino to be an honest man. In fact, there has never been the slightest breath of scandal about his private life.

It was plain that friendship or kinship, and not true merit, had placed many in high places where they did not belong. It was only rumored at first that some of these were using their exalted positions as looting posts, for which the people paid. And there was loot on every hand to be had for the taking in the Philippines for those who had the power to take it, even if they lacked the right.

On each trip home I grew more bewildered. How had we managed to get into such a mess, and in so short a time? Why were the Filipinos, who had fought to a man for their freedom, now fighting amongst themselves after having won that freedom?

To those who criticized from afar it was not easy to explain that while the Philippines had been launched into independence in an extravagant love feast of good wishes and good will, actually our little country was operating under handicaps that would have ruined a far larger, richer, and more experienced nation.

Even the task of the shift in leadership was a difficult one.

A nation owes its greatness in large measure to its great men, and we had been fortunate in our leaders. It was tragic that we lost our two greatest in times of crisis when they were most needed. The prophet of the modern Filipino struggle for nationhood was and still is the late Manuel Luis Quezon. He was the revolutionary leader par excellence, and more than that, he was the man the people trusted as their champion when the struggle moved from the battlefield to the debating floor.

Quezon dominated the Philippine scene from the days of the Revolution of 1900 to the middle of the Second World War when he died in 1944. His patriotism and his devotion to the people and to the nation will always be beyond question. But the very intensity of Quezon's patriotism and his consciousness of his own worth and his own loyalty moved him to construct in the Philippine political scene an edifice in which loyalty was primarily to the political party, which in his hands had become the powerful weapon that brought independence to his country. Quezon built his party around himself and chose his own aides, whom he trained to succeed him and help guide the nation. Among these was Manuel Roxas.

The loyalty Quezon stood for was a personal loyalty, since he identified himself with the true interests of the nation. To this identification he gave everything—at the last, his health and his life. But it was not an institutional loyalty, and it was bound to be weakened in any case with the passing of Quezon.

When his death occurred in the midst of a destructive enemy occupation, the weakness of the political structure was revealed. It took place at a time when the iron rule of Japanese military power was clamped down over the archipelago, and particularly on our political institutions. During that time only the men Quezon had taught and trained in the inadequate concept of individual loyalty remained to lead.

That they led patriotically and in most cases self-sacrificingly is beyond question. But that their very training was for loyalty to a personality and to a concept of leadership rather than to the democratic principle of the people's innermost feelings and convictions, later events were to prove only too well.

For throughout the occupation it was the Filipinos themselves who resisted the enemy. It was the people who gave their fullest proof of loyalty to democracy, and the people who remained steadfast to the principles given to them by America, while the leaders, perhaps with a more farsighted outlook, or with the hope of protecting their people from further atrocities—since if they protested they would be replaced—did not go along with the people in and out of resistance. It was the people, rather than the leaders, who gave the most convincing proof of their devotion to the basic tenets of democracy and their readiness to sacrifice all—as many did—in support of these tenets, and who saw in the American internees at Santo Tomas, in Bilibid and in Los Baños, and the American refugees they hid and protected, living symbols of democracy under trial. It was the people of the Philippines who flung themselves and all they possessed into the struggle against the invaders, while their counterparts in Asia, the people of Thailand, Burma, Indonesia, and others, were, to put it mildly, at least indifferent to the invading Japanese and their activities.

It is not difficult to trace this devotion on the Filipinos' part to the democratic principle, insofar as that principle is based on the freedom of the individual, which is something the Japanese conquerer rejected from the start. There is no place in the Japanese code of *Bushido* for the rights of the individual. But in the Philippines this pride in self goes far back—far beyond the better-trained and the more cultured outlook of the modern leaders—to the libertarian ideals of the Filipino rebels who first challenged Spanish power.

Before the turn of the century, José Rizal, the man who was to be hailed as the voice of Filipino freedom, wrote a novel which in its sphere and within its orientation had all the impact of Rousseau's *Le Contrat Social* and Thomas Paine's *The Age of Reason*. This book was titled *The Reign of Greed,* and in it the author sounded a call against social corruption which was to be echoed in the memorable "Cry of Balintawak"—this actually was the defiant act of tearing up the Spanish tax papers at the town of Balintawak—a cry which to the Filipino has all the significance of the shot the Concord farmers fired "where the arched bridge spans the flood."

That cry overthrew Spain in the Philippines.

The devotion to the freedom that is democracy goes back then in the Philippines to Rizal; to Andres Bonifacio, who led the first embattled revolt against the corrupt and tyrannical Spanish regime; to Aguinaldo, who consolidated the revolution against the United States that had taken us over from Spain. It also goes back to the devoted "Thousand"—the one thousand American teachers who came to the Philippines on the transport *Thomas* at the turn of the century—who came not only to teach, but to learn from the people with whom they had cast their lot. The Thomasites worked and lived with the Filipinos as the Filipinos themselves worked and lived. They taught, not by carping and by critical precept, but by living, arduous, and ardent example.

From Rizal to the Thomasites, all had worked hard to plant the seeds of democracy at the base of our social pyramid. The seeds struck root, not alone among the leaders at the top, but amongst the people. So when the great test came to the Philippines and the Japanese invaders imprisoned the nation for three-and-a-half terrible years, it was the people imbued with the basic ideals of democracy who resisted, and who during the process of resistance developed new and younger leaders, with new concepts of leadership, and with an approach to the real problems of these trying times that was entirely new.

It was also during the years of the resistance that old

and new, aged and young, met in opposition and failed to understand one another.

So the war had ended, leaving behind whatever had been attained in building a democracy in the Philippines founded on the major premise of the rights of the individual, and leaving the country itself, like all the rest of the Asian mainland, in the shambles of general overthrow. In the Philippines the very force of the resistance movement, which had spent itself in the effort to preserve the essence of this democracy in captivity, had served to weaken its bases by weakening the factor without which this true democracy can neither be conceived nor endure: the factor of orderly, lawful process.

Youth was in the saddle now, having learned its own importance in war. Youth was made restless by the mundane necessity of earning a living after the excitement of war.

For three-and-a-half years our young men had carried on warfare against a ruthless enemy. To deceive and kill in order to survive was a lesson they had learned only too well and during the most impressionable period of their lives. They were accustomed to live without restriction or authority and by jungle law.

To a generation of young Filipinos, who, like their *maquis* counterparts in Western Europe, had cut their teeth on commando knives and been weaned on the bitter pabulum of hatred, it was right and praiseworthy to take from the invader and to kill in the taking. The beneficent influence of the Catholic Church in which the vast majority of these youths had been raised softened the harsher aspects of this new outlook on life, but it could not alter

81

the essential demands of the exigency of that life. The invader with his *zona*—the zones designated by the Japanese wherein every Filipino male became a prisoner—his night searches, his roundups and torture sessions and mass executions, was lawful prey. The Filipino's arms were the arms of the guerrillas until American guns began pouring into the country. His rice was the food of a starving, oppressed but by no means defeated people. He knew no process of law, therefore process of law was shelved on both sides.

On this note the war ended, and the guns had not long been stilled on the last Philippine fighting fronts—along the Shimbu line east of Manila, in the steep ridge lands of the Santa Fe, in the jungles of Mindanao—when democracy in the Philippines began to show the first symptoms of postcombat disease.

Philippine democracy, the strongest and the healthiest democracy on the western side of the Pacific, had been dealt a body blow. It had been attacked in its most vital elements, of which the major ingredients are first the individual's concept of his obligation to his neighbor, and secondly, those processes of law which experience has evolved through the centuries to enforce this obligation, and which the Filipinos had inherited ready-made from the Constitution and the underlying principles of the United States.

To make the situation after the surrender even more dangerous, there were not lacking in the Philippines self-seeking men, who cannot be classified exclusively by race, who saw in the moral dissolution spawned by the war-born disregard for law and order a means for their own enrichment.

There was plenty of material with which to advance their plans. The postwar country lay lush and ready for the miasmatic growth of corruption. In the midst of chaos, the newly born Philippine Republic was trying to put into working order an honest, fair, and efficient form of government.

The position of the country and the government could hardly have been worse. The Japanese invader had been destroyed, but in the last vicious struggle for survival and in sheer wanton vengeance he had destroyed much of the country's resources. Public buildings were rubble heaps, money was gone, records were burned or lost, schools had vanished, and the roads of which we had been so justly proud were at best tracks of smashed asphalt and at worst rutted lanes under tangled jungle growth.

Saddest of all, the morale of the people was at a record low.

They were discouraged and poor, and all around them was plenty.

The island of Luzon was a vast warehouse containing the greatest store of military supplies and armaments ever brought together, once destined for the maintenance of the mightiest army ever assembled. General MacArthur had planned a major invasion of Japan from our shores, and the sudden collapse of Japan had left billions of dollars' worth of food, military equipment, and construction materials, not to mention arms and ammunition, stored in a chain of warehouses stretching the length of the archipelago.

This vast reservoir of goods could not as a matter of practical operation be returned to the United States. Much of it, if not all, could be of use in rebuilding the shattered economy of the new Republic of the Philippines, which celebrated its first birthday less than eleven months after the surrender.

A policy, basically wise, was established by the United States: all this war surplus was to be handed over to the government of the Philippines. Sales to private individuals would be conducted by the government and the proceeds were to serve as the base for the economic program of the new Republic.

On paper the plan was excellent. With any sort of law and order prevailing, with any means of curbing the greed of the unscrupulous, it would have worked, and the new nation would have been off to a splendid start. Unfortunately, before the plan could be put into effect, the schemes of less scrupulous people moved faster. Cupidity was aroused by this unexampled massing of wealth and sources for more wealth, and it was abetted by the nation-wide lapse from essential moral values engendered by the years of resistance against a foe who knew neither morals nor law. Actually, the enormous surplus stores had been left abandoned under the most tenuous of regulations, which were enforced poorly or not at all by venal officials, both American and Filipino. There was wealth for the taking by all who could gain access to the surplus stores —and many did, by connivance from both sides.

Thus, the barriers were let down for the most flagrant grabbing and grafting in what was actually national property, and the result was the widely publicized and infamous "surplus scandals." The "smart money boys" (and there were girls among them, too, who got their share!) were those who during the war had done the least toward resisting the enemy, but they had managed to retain the keys to social friendship and to political influence. They knew they had but little time. They knew that the people's basic awareness of their rights and their perhaps violent reaction to those who would rob them of their heritage could not be long held down or delayed. So the greedy ones worked fast, and the result was an unprecedented wave of prosperity for the few. Mansions and palaces sprang up as if by magic from the ruins of the occupation and war. Expensive cars rolled down streets and roads still marred with combat shellfire that no money could be found to repair, although for other purposes money flowed in an apparently endless stream. We had the equivalent of the mink coats, champagne briberies, and five percenters! And always the trail led to high places in the government and in politics, because it was there that the source of the easy concessions of favored deals in surplus property could be found.

When it is remembered that these stores were to have been used as the foundations in the rebuilding of the country's economic structure, it is apparent how great was the disaster and how heavy were the handicaps placed on the Philippines and the great mass of its people, who had asked only for opportunity to return to their fields and sow and harvest there and rebuild their shattered huts.

Now this dream was changed by the mirage of sudden wealth. Why slave under the hot sun behind a sweating carabao when others were making fortunes overnight?

To another degree, but under the same principle, the United States had experienced a similar nightmare in the lush months of the 1928-1929 boom, when work was at a discount while fortunes could be made gambling on margin. It had taken a world-shaking depression to jolt the American people back to the sobering realization that citizens can live and prosper only by putting something into a country before they attempt to take anything out of it.

It would take the Filipinos seven years and the threat of revolution before they would finally test and find wanting the "get-rich-quick" way of life.

Considering the vast amount of wealth involved, and the debacle and confusion in the postwar Philippines, the wonder is not that there was graft and malversation of goods and funds, but that there was not more.

But the surplus scandal was only one aspect of the general moral collapse. It marked the beginning of a reign of greed and graft—and the start of the weakening of popular faith in the government.

The honest and devoted political leaders were forced back before the onslaught of the forces of greed. Fortunes continued to mushroom overnight by the operation of the most flagrant graft and incompetence in government levels, both low and high. Inevitably, this infected the thinking of the people. Their faith turned to a general distrust of the government as it existed, and then, inevitably, it turned to a dangerous public distrust of the values of that democracy which the Filipino people had been taught to trust and to fight for since the days of José Rizal.

For how could a citizen be expected to believe in a

representative government when the man he had helped elect to represent him in Congress was named as one who accepted bribes, and whose relatives were growing richer at every tick of the clock?

Every letdown in the honor and strength of the government was matched by a weakening of faith in democracy. Certainly the Filipinos, if they were not quite ready to abandon democracy as a way of life, were ready to discard a government which was giving increasing daily evidence of its incapacity to maintain the essence of the democratic processes, to deal honestly with its people, and to fulfill its most important function of protecting its people from abuse.

This was their mood in that dangerous year 1949 when China fell.

Elsewhere in Asia, where democracy had never existed or where it had died, Communism had taken over.

In the Philippines, democracy started on its slow and agonizing death. Here was the chance the secret enemy within had wanted. Perfectly synchronized with the governmental curve of graft and corruption in our struggling new Republic was the Communists' rise to power.

Their big chance came with the so-called "dirty election" of '49.

The "reign of greed" which Rizal had used as a lever to loosen entrenched tyranny in 1898 could have taken lessons from the reign of greed which the monstrous parody on free elections perpetrated in 1949. In this year Quirino came up for election, having become president before not by election but by the death of Roxas. In the national election which will be remembered by us as the "crooked" or "dirty" election, a President, a Vice President, senators, representatives, and scores of other officials were "chosen" by fraudulent practices that wrote a new record of sordidness into the history of politics.

Intimidation and fraud would be proven later, and one asks, do such exposés hurt or help? The answer is—they must be made. The sore must be opened to be cleansed. The intimidation was obvious at the time. The Huks wanted the Liberal Party to stay in power. In every section of the archipelago hired gangsters armed with tommy guns and rifles taken from United States army supplies patrolled the streets and guarded the polls, firing into the air at intervals to frighten away those who were not members of the Liberal Party. Thousands of would-be voters were terrified and stayed in their homes: they did not vote. Others tried and were driven back. Many hundreds were killed.

But the Liberals cast their votes to the last man—and beyond that. In Negros and in Lanao, two provinces in the south, there were more votes cast than there were registered voters.

We made a sour joke about these election returns: "Obviously, even the bees and birds and the cadavers in the cemeteries voted." But the grimness of the jest was indicative of the moral breakdown in the government to which had been entrusted the maintenance of a bitterly won democracy.

It would take too long to recount the whole story of that swindling of the people in the "dirty election" of 1949 that gave the "get-rich-quick boys" around Quirino their biggest chance at the great national robbery. It is sufficient here to affirm, with all the evidence needed and more to support the statement, if necessary, that a regime which had countenanced, and in some ways abetted, the wholesale rape of the nation's economic resources in the immediate postwar years was perpetuated in power by the most flagrant abuse of elections, and by the most callous and contemptuous disregard of the people's rights, aspirations, and hopes.

The Huks controlled that election, which almost succeeded in turning the Philippines over to the Soviets. This bald prostitution of the popular ballot; the deliberate misuse of governmental facilities by the Quirino regime and its power-greedy supporters, in and out of office; the shameless stuffing of ballot boxes and the recruitment of the heavily-armed goon squads to intimidate and if necessary assault would-be voters—all this had but one objective, to place in the hands of the perpetrators of this monstrous plot what amounted to virtually complete control of the wealth of the Philippines and of property belonging to the Filipino people.

For half a century we had waited for the privilege of casting our votes as free citizens of an independent nation. The election of 1949 robbed us of that right and desecrated popular suffrage that meant so much to us.

The faith of the people was undermined. So this was democracy!

The result was growing hatred and distrust by the people against the government in power. Every fraudulent vote cast in the "dirty election" added to the lengthening shadow of Communism falling across the Philippines.

89

Chapter VI

RAPID strides carried the Filipinos from freedom into terrorism.

The "dirty election" of 1949 opened the country to graft; graft opened the country to the Communists. It was as simple as that.

Directly following the election, the "get-rich-quick lads" were embarked on the campaign of looting which spared nothing remotely available through government or political connections. There was nothing left when they finished gathering the riches which governmental influence at best, and active corruption at worst, placed at their disposal.

The excess wealth lying about uncounted, plus lack of moral authority, combined to bring about this wholesale looting of the nation. The major perpetrators were out to get as much as they could while there was anything left to grab, and those who became the overnight millionaires were the closest to those in the high places. The common people were left with nothing.

All departments of the government permitted the most brazen examples of nepotism and of favoritism and the most flagrant abuse of the public trust. Relatives of high officials trafficked openly in favors, in licenses for imports on which the lifeblood of the nation's trade depended, and in the property placed at the disposal of the Philippine government by the United States.

The effect of such widespread corruption on the treasury was only what could have been expected. Trust funds were looted. Teachers' salaries remained unpaid for months. Even postal funds were not safe.

There were many sincere, honest, patriotic men in the government. They were helpless, but not silenced. The major leaders of the opposition—Dr. José P. Laurel, Claro M. Recto, Eulogio "Amang" Rodriguez, the venerable president of the senate, and Vice President Fernando Lopez of the Liberal Party, and many others missed no opportunity to expose and attack the administration. Senator Lorenzo Tañada of the Citizens' Party played an important role in assailing the Quirino regime for its corruption.

Fortunately for the Filipinos, we have developed a press which is one of the freest in the world. A rigid libel law never operated to prevent the harshest exposures of corruption. The evils of the government were constantly held up before the public. The weekly magazine, *Philippines Free Press,* was in the forefront of this campaign.

In Washington, I read in the newspapers and in the *Reader's Digest* and *Saturday Evening Post* and other magazines, exposés of the corruption and graft in the Philippines, and I had no answers for those whose questioning became acute, for they were based on facts I knew to be true. Letters I received from relatives and friends at home corroborated the published exposés and let me know the truth behind the propaganda sent me from Malacañan.

No one was being spared by the crusaders, as scandal after scandal was aired.

Among the worst examples of graft and corruption was the Chinese Immigration Scandal. We have a law in the Philippines limiting the entry of Chinese immigrants. Unbeknown to the people, each member of the Congress and Senate is "entitled" to grant entry to five Chinese. Naturally, with the troubles in China pressing at their heels, Chinese were very anxious to enter the Philippines, and it was discovered that some of the wealthy could be persuaded to pass as much as one hundred thousand pesos "under the counter" for the privilege. Five times that sum amounted to half a million pesos each for our solons.

No wonder our politicians were getting rich!

This racket was exposed by Vice President Lopez shortly after the 1949 election. He was a member of the party in power, but he had the honesty and courage to admit it could be wrong.

The next exposure concerned the Maria Cristina hydroelectric power installation to be built by the government. The project had been farmed out without bids to an Italian contractor. This too was exposed by Lopez, and as a result the contract was canceled, bids were ordered, and the contract was given to Westinghouse.

Under the original contract the people would have lost a great deal.

Other scandals burst around Malacañan like fireworks.

It was public knowledge that the Bureau of Customs was riddled with graft. Merchants were substituting the payment of duty with bribes. It was cheaper that way and the only way goods could be handled; without the palm-greasing there would be loss, damage, and delay.

The Import Control Commission was shot through with corruption. A businessman had to grease certain official palms to get his license to import and keep them greased to bring goods in or ship them out.

Then there was the scandal over the Philippine National Bank, an official of which with influence in high places had been given a loan of more than three million pesos—without collateral!

The evils of the government were constantly held up before the public. But between exposure and remedy a wide gulf remained. It was plain that certain people very close to the administration kept on receiving millions.

One result became more noticeable: the definite fall in the people's confidence in the government. It was now that the swelling force that was Communism entered the gap which lay between a people's faith and their loss of faith. It was this evil year of 1949 and its "dirty election" that brought the Communists out in the open in the Philippines and started them on their rise to power.

The Huks or "HMB" were the military spearhead of the Communist forces in our country. These were the members of the Hukbalahap, or, to give the organization its full formal designation, the "Hukbong Magpapalaya ng Bayan," or "Army of Liberation of the People." Its origins were in the embryonic Communist Party of the Philippines which had been organized in the early thirties by Pedro Abad Santos and his aides.

During the Japanese invasion the Huk elements had organized under that name into the most effective guerrilla units operating against the invaders. But the story of the Huk movement goes far back beyond World War II, and it was always based on the precept of hatred of the existing government.

It began in the early '20's in the poorly populated areas of Central Luzon, where a few wealthy and often absentee landlords paid no attention to the agrarian unrest amongst the people, who had too little land to support their needs and no one to represent them. The government had made half-hearted attempts to provide bits of land that would in turn furnish a living for those in need, but the efforts never matured, and as a result deeper resentment was born. The mutterings of protest were turned by the Soviet converts into arguments in favor of Communism, and out of the individual desire for a bit of land to call one's own came a group desire to take all the land and redistribute it according to Communistic dictates; in other words— here was the first talk of revolution.

When Japan struck in 1941, the Huks had organized into fighting groups.

World War II and its resultant upheaval helped spread the Red propaganda, for where, the leaders demanded, was American aid, and how had democracy helped the Filipino? Nothing could be done to offset such a movement then, for everyone was busy fighting the Japanese, and it must be admitted that among the most valiant were the Huks, the scattered Communists organized now under that name into a large, although diffused, military force.

But they were fighting against Japan, not for democracy.

The end of the war found the Huks a large, powerful

94

and discontented group, well armed with American guns and other armament that had been smuggled into the country by submarine during the war, or taken by the Huks from the Japanese they had captured. Along with this armament went enough ammunition to see them through any war they might devise.

They were on their own now and out in the open. They had never been friendly with the other guerrilla groups who had fought for democracy. There had always been between the two factions that tension which bespoke the real objective of the Huks, the establishment of a Soviet Communist regime in the Philippines.

Their new leaders were Luis Taruc, the supreme Huk who had been forced out of politics in Manila as a Communist, and his principal aides, Casto Alejandrino, Guillermo Capadocia, Balgos and others. None of these was ever avowedly "Soviet Communist." They were always "agrarian reformers," bent on getting the poor "tao" his bit of land and his place in the sun, and they never admitted that their military units operated along lines tested and approved by their Comintern masters, and that the orders they mouthed or published in their pamphlets and periodic "press releases" were cliches which were the demands of the moment from the party line in Moscow.

The question is often asked how a movement like that of the Huks, which was essentially Communist in motivation and indoctrination, could prosper in a country in which eighty per cent of the population are Catholic. The answer is simple. The "hard core" of the movement, the indoctrinated and dedicated leaders, had learned their lessons in excellent schools for Communism (some in the very shadow of the Kremlin). These "experts" never made the mistake of introducing the atheistic angle into the propaganda they were infiltrating into the peasant masses of Central Luzon, although this was a region tailored for Communism through generations of absentee landlordism —of feudal rule by religious orders and subsequently by owners of the vast estates formerly owned by the orders. But never once did the Huk leaders admit, to Luzon or to the outer world, that they were Soviet-propelled. They were simply the saviors of a simple and oppressed people —no more.

This was how they won the attention and raised the ebbing hopes of the people who had expected so much when war ended and were given little or nothing. The scandals in the government, the betrayal of the public vote in the "dirty election," were tools the Communists used with Kremlin-taught skill to bring themselves to power. The Huks were exploiting and magnifying everything, and spreading propaganda by printed word and from mouth to mouth to inflame the people against a political regime which was failing them, and which the Huks cited as the failure of democracy.

Now they were organizing against the government men who had fought for democracy and who had been ready to die that this very government might survive!

It was a familiar pattern. This was the way it had been done in China. This was the pattern that had betrayed China so that in this very year China fell.

The Huks formed themselves into bandit bands. They were joined by a lost generation of young men who had been taught to rob and kill in war that change might come to better their land—and there had been no change.

They were joined, too, by a scattering of criminals who had fled under sentence or been released by the Japanese during the invasion. Rapists, killers, lawbreakers of every kind were to be found in the Red forces organized by the Huks to harry, subdue, or argue the bewildered peasants into meek acceptance of the rapidly advancing Red authority.

So the Huks succeeded in subduing the people where the Japanese had failed. Aided and abetted by their greatest ally, corruption in high places, which brought increasing conviction to the people that their government was not worth defending, the Huks continued to grow in strength and numbers, under the protection of the people, who began providing food and protection for the Huks, not through fear, but because of their own despair.

Actually, the military force of the Huks was never overwhelming. On Luzon their estimated strength at its height consisted of twenty thousand well-armed men, and Magsaysay was later to estimate the all-over organization at sixty thousand. Out of a population of twenty-one million this is not a large number, but Red conquest never starts with large numbers. We had seen the Red stain spread over White Russia and had learned not to underestimate the power of the minority.

The real danger was the mood of the people. The strength of the Huk movement around Manila lay in the tacit, sometimes active, and always willing support given the Huks by nearly two hundred thousand peasants in the teeming rice fields of Central Luzon.

The Huk leaders were far too clever and too well trained in the finesse of infiltration to attempt open revolt by all the peasants. They worked rather by indirection. They organized the peasantry in supply sections, as their prototypes had done in China. They trained eligible men in simple governmental duties and maneuvered them into state positions, so that it was not long before practically every important town in Luzon, not excluding Manila, had literally a "standby government," ready to take over—when the Red uprising began—the functions of mayor and local councils and to supplant the official police forces; ready, in short, to assume the functions of government with full control of all communication facilities, from the wire telegraph to the radio.

By 1950 the Huks had reached the height of power and were moving at will about the land, spreading through many islands, and even into the remote southern regions. Corruption in the government reached an all-time high, and the prestige of the government sank to its all-time low. Government credit had reached the vanishing point, there were rumors of the collapse of the peso, and bitterest of all to remember was the two billion dollars given to the people by America with which to aid and bring to maturity the fledgling Republic; gone, along with the last of our own resources, into the maw of government-protected greed. In cities and in the country the Red terrorists roamed at will, equipped by this time with the bounteous supply of ammunition laid up in our country against the invasion of Japan, and which had been permitted by crooked dealings to fall almost entirely into their hands. It is needlessly laboring a point to suggest that the Huks were being supplied with Red arms from the Asian mainland by junk or submarine. They needed no such help from their Soviet masters. Munitions that but for criminal neglect in high places would have been safely stored in the government arsenals were by this time stored in inaccessible hoards in the jungles and hills of Luzon. To the bitter end the "hard core" recalcitrants among the Huks would not surrender their American arms because they knew they possessed an almost inexhaustible supply of American ammunition to fit those arms.

All over the archipelago were panic and the fearful wait that precedes change. The countryside was deserted and in the barrios the huts stood empty and desolate. Farmers no longer farmed. The rice crops lay waste, and the people were hungry. The villagers fled to the cities. In Manila the Politburo set up its headquarters in fine Communist tradition, with the Huk leaders in charge, and were laying definite plans to take first Malacañan and the President, then the entire city. In Manila there was terror in the streets and there were areas where people dared not venture by night for fear of the marauding bands of Huks. The Huks had a well-publicized plan: a membership of two million in another year and then—they would possess the Philippines!

Democracy in the Philippines was on its deathbed, and the Communist-Huk forces were preparing for the *coup de grâce*.

All this was known to the regular forces of the government. At this stage even the most lackadaisical "high brass" of the armed forces admitted that they expected the worst. President Quirino was under heavy guard and in constant fear of his life. It was only a question of time until the Huks took over.

The question may be asked that everyone was asking then: "Why does not someone stop them? Why are they not stopped—in time?"

And the answer to that is that by the time such a movement reaches its climax there is no one left strong enough to protest.

What had happened to our constabulary, of which we had been so justly proud? And where was our army that had fought so long and ably against the Japanese? Why hadn't they stopped the Huks in their tracks, in the beginning? Why weren't they stopping them now?

The story of what had happened to our police and to our soldiers is one other of the tragic chapters in this history of a dying democracy. The sad truth is that by this time the people hated and feared the soldiers and the police even more than they did the Huks.

A few days before the attaining of our independence the Philippines received the command of thirty-seven thousand officers and men, turned over to it by the United States. This was the Armed Forces of the Republic, originally organized into about seventeen thousand members of the army, navy, and air force which had training and routine peacetime missions under the Department of National Defense, and twenty thousand members of the constabulary, our national police force, under the authority of the Department of the Interior.

The police force was entrusted with the mission of restoring peace and order. The Huks came under their jurisdiction in the beginning, since the first activities of the Huks consisted of murder, robbery, rape, kidnapping, extortion, and other crimes that were obviously problems for the police.

The Huks were too well organized and too well armed to be cowed by our postwar constabulary, which was, to be frank, a hastily organized and ineffective group with little or no training in police work, so different from the efficient prewar constabulary force. The municipal police were helpless, and their attempts to subdue the Huks were futile.

The people gave little support to the local police in their abortive attempts to establish law and order. They were too disapproving of their government to want to help any more in any way.

So by this year 1950 the government officials had every reason to be alarmed. At first they had blandly regarded the disturbance as the settling-down process. Now they belatedly recognized at last the Huk movement for what it was—a carefully planned all-over plot to seize national power.

Obviously, this threat was no longer a scattering of desperate incidents fit only for police blotters. It was a national menace, and only the army could protect the Filipinos now—provided it was not too late.

President Quirino issued stern orders to the army: "Clean out the Huks!"

And the Philippine Army, whose men had displayed battlefield capacity that had made them the equal of any fighting men in the world, lay down on the job. They, too, had been allowed to drift in the general letdown of the Republic. Here too was influence, nepotism, greed. Officers were activated and deactivated without any regard to their ability or their service records, but rather to their family and political connections and above all to their "services" to the party entrenched in power in Malacañan and the regime which ruled it.

Periodic "campaigns" were launched against the "dissidents," as the Huks were known, but these were farcical maneuvers in which a few troops would announce weeks in advance their next objective, and on that occasion would deploy at the base of specified hills and there fire a few hundred rounds of expensive ammunition (the army did not have as great a supply of ammunition as did the Huks) into the jungle where they were sure to hurt no one. Then they would retire, with great tales of Huk dead.

Even when the target was not announced in advance, someone always knew, and the Huks were warned in advance.

It soon became plain that the army was not interested in bringing the Huks to heel. Battlewise officers, trained and experienced in combat and willing to put up an earnest fight to save the country, were deliberately sidetracked by political manipulators, while units they had trained to fight most effectively were broken up and distributed among other formations.

Only four year before, the little Republic of the Philippines had started out so bravely as the frontier of democracy in the Far East. We were to have been the "show window" of democracy in Asia.

Now the blueprint of aggression had been fitted over the Philippines from within with the aid of a weak, inept, and graft-ridden government. This year of 1950 found the country helplessly facing revolution, with the Huks ready to take over when the Republic fell.

And still it was in this same year that Filipino soldiers were fighting and dying in the effort to preserve democracy on the blood-drenched ridges of Korea, and the Philippine Republic was making every effort to fulfill its obligations to the democratic concept in the international field.

On the world front every effort was being made to establish the peace that had been won by war. But there was no peace in Korea, China, Malaya, and Indochina. There was no peace in the Philippines.

In this year President Quirino asked me to interrupt my battlings with Andrei Vishinsky in the United Nations to organize and serve as Chief Delegate of the Philippines to the first Southeast Asia Conference in the Philippines. Seven nations met at Baguio, our summer resort—India, Thailand, Ceylon, Pakistan, Australia, Indonesia, the Philippines. I went from door to door in Washington in the attempt to find help in the movement to unite Asia; I was cold-shouldered. No one in Washington seemed to see any importance then in such a meeting of minds in Asia. Several American leaders said, "It's impractical. It can't be done."

In four more years those very men would be working frantically against time in a belated effort to achieve a similar organization among the few Asian nations that remained free.

If only we had succeeded then! Indochina would have been saved.

On my trips across the Pacific I caught increasingly dis-

103

turbing glimpses of what was going on in the Philippines, so when in this same year President Quirino asked me to return to Manila as his Secretary of Foreign Affairs, I readily accepted the portfolio. My battles with Vishinsky in the United Nations had made me so aware of the Soviet danger that I welcomed the chance to help fight Communism on the home front.

Chapter VII

THE many battles against the chromium-plated "realism" of the Russian delegates to the United Nations might have prepared me for the danger of challenging entrenched Communism in the Philippines. Unfortunately, this was not so. I was not prepared for the advances they had made, and the open way they were flaunting their intentions and their ability to carry them out.

Even the atrocities committed by the Japanese had not prepared me for the atrocities Filipinos were perpetrating on their brother Filipinos under the Red flag. The Red propagandists had done a thorough job of splitting the Republic. Filipinos who had not been subdued by terrorism had been wooed by pledges of protection or future privileges, once the Huks took over. Beyond these was the dead sea of the lethargic who had ceased to care.

It seemed inconceivable to me that men who had fought side by side on Bataan and Corregidor could have been turned into enemies tearing at one another's throats, and in so short a time. But that is the power of Communism. It knows how to blank out all reason and leave only hatred. It knows how to twist and befoul. All this had been done without actual Russian intervention. It was not needed. The Filipino disciples of the Red terror were doing a superb job.

The Communists had a Black List of those they intended to kill as being enemies of the Huk ideal. President Quirino and Vice President Lopez led the list as the arch opponents of Communism within the Philippines, and I learned that mine was the honor of being number three on the list because I had been one of the chief antagonists of Vishinsky in the United Nations.

It was not the first time I had been on such a list. In the tunnel on Corregidor I had listened to the Japanese broadcasts proclaiming a price on my head because of the work I was doing on the "Voice of Freedom," broadcasting to the captive mainland from the tunnel. This time, my brother Filipinos had put me on the death list.

I drove through a Manila still in ruins and under threat of siege, to the Palace which was also alerted and under heavy guard. President Quirino was virtually a prisoner behind the tall walls of Malacañan. He and his staff were drilled to escape the palace by secret ways in case of attack. Out in the middle of Manila Bay his yacht rocked at anchor under heavy guard. He had been warned not to board it, as the Huks had planned an attack with small craft if he did, with the intent of capturing the yacht and taking the President prisoner.

Every day the threat of eruption grew in Manila. The police and soldiers and palace guards were trying to keep down trouble, but their attempts seemed half-hearted and no one knew what might happen at any moment. It was like the hours after Pearl Harbor when we had gone about our affairs always with an eye on the skies to see if the

Japanese were about to attack. Now people went about their business nervously, and night life, that had been a joyous matter in prewar Manila, consisted of brief visits to restaurants or homes, because everyone was anxious to get in before curfew. Yes, we had curfew; after six you could not drive out of the city at all.

By day, at stated points of entry into the city, incomers were searched to make certain they were not carrying arms, but this was futile protection since Manila was a common storehouse of arms and ammunition.

The city was crowded with refugees, and all around us was poverty and despair. The word "Huks" had become one to inspire fear.

I drove into the country, through areas laid waste by the Huk marauders, where crops had been reaped or burned and livestock driven off to feed their armies. From the ash heaps that had been homes, burned by the Huks, the villagers and farmers had fled into the cities, creating the growing problem of destitution that was just one more terrible problem our dying Republic had to face. The peasants I spoke to were destitute, or they were protecting, and therefore being protected by, the Huks.

That was the answer. The Huks made promises or spread terror. There was no compromise. Accept Communism or die!

And the government these people had expected to serve as their protector and their shield lacked the will and the strength now to keep them alive. Graft had sucked away its power. Corruption had rotted away its strength. Every fine house built on pilfered gains stolen from the people, every bribe taken by officials high or low, every jewel and imported car flaunted by the newly rich, was fuel added to the holocaust that was consuming our Republic.

The grafters could pretend to ignore the fact that their hands were stained with blood. The Huks knew exactly what they were doing, and did it with a sadism that had the archipelago cowering in fear. With increasing insolence they continued to sweep through the islands burning and pillaging, kidnapping, robbing, raping, killing. No crime was too great or too small, or too wickedly senseless. Nothing the Japanese had done to us was as senselessly cruel.

In the capital of my own province of Tarlac they swarmed down on the hospital one night and killed over fifty nurses and their patients. From some of the nurses they removed the eyes.

Of all the acts of this reign of terror the most senseless was the murder of Doña Aurora Quezon, the widow of our martyred President, Manuel Quezon. The day before, she had invited me to ride with the family in motorcade to Baler, where a monument to her dead husband was to be unveiled. It hurt me to say no to this gentle friend but I was leaving the next day on a rush trip to the United States.

In Honolulu, the next day, I picked up a newspaper between planes and saw the headline: MRS. QUEZON AMBUSHED.

She and her daughter Maria Aurora, and Felipe Buencamino III who was the husband of her other daughter, and Ponciano Bernardo who was the Mayor of Quezon City, good people all, had been surrounded on the road and blasted out of existence by a band of Huks.

That was all we have ever learned about the mass murder, that it had been planned and committed by Huks. We have never learned the reason for the killings, and there may have been no reason. There are many guesses, to be sure. Some think the Huks had been told President Quirino was to be in the car. Others are convinced the act was committed by men who hated the very memory of Quezon because he had emblematized for us democracy, while others believe that the Huk killers had hoped the death of almost all the late President's family might bring about a division of lands in Arayat and Pampanga, where the Quezons had holdings.

We shall probably never know the truth.

I read the story of the ambush on the airfield at Honolulu and remembered the bravery and the goodness of Aurora Quezon in the tunnel on Corregidor where she had lived underground with her President-husband during the siege of the Philippines. I remembered her after one of the many air raids that had blasted the Rock, walking down the tunnels that smelled of gangrene and human filth, and bending over the wounded American and Filipino boys who lay on their stretchers in the fetid gloom. She had a sweet smile and an encouraging word for each one, before she would turn away to hide the tears. Later, after escaping from the Rock by submarine with her President-husband and her children, she had seen her husband die for democracy, and still later, she had seen the birth of the Philippine Republic.

Now she had been butchered on a country road, the innocent victim of the Huk gangsters who were determined to destroy the Republic for which her husband had lived, and had given his life. She who had never taken part in politics had joined him in martyrdom.

The memory of Quezon holds for Filipinos all that the memory of George Washington holds for the Americans, and his birthday is celebrated by us as a national holiday. In Manila there is also a large parade. Let me give one example of the way the Huks had infiltrated into every echelon of the government, no matter how high. One Quezon Day, President Quirino and his highest dignitaries with a full display of military brass were reviewing the parade from the grandstand, when suddenly, no one knew how, we all found ourselves passing pamphlets from hand to hand. Looking at them, we burst into excited talk.

Who had started passing out the leaflets?

We never found out.

They were Huk propaganda pamphlets carrying printed charges against the Quirino administration and the Constitution, and naming names and listing all the government scandals from the National Bank Scandal on down. Many of those in the group around the President read their names on the Huk list.

We never learned who smuggled the pamphlets into the reviewing stand, but it must have been one of us in the President's own inner circle.

Wherever one turned, there were Communists. They wore many faces and took many forms, but under the surface was the deadly determination of the Moscow-trained.

I have written of Roberto, the bright young man I had selected from many students in Manila to work with me on temporary assignment in the Philippine Mission in New York. He had been with me in New Delhi, Geneva, Rome,

Paris and other cities, and later had asked to be returned to Manila. Now as Secretary of Foreign Affairs I was glad to have him again under my jurisdiction, and versed as he was in foreign affairs, he proved to be of the utmost usefulness, although his position was still unofficial. He was bright and willing and had a wide grasp of all the problems that faced our department, and before long, as earlier, he became my valued unofficial aide. He was indispensable during the Southeast Asia Conference at Baguio. Equally indispensable was another young man I will call Manuel, a friend of Roberto, whom he had brought to my office, very strongly recommending him as a valuable assistant I might find especially useful on my official trips abroad.

Both had been with me at Baguio during the Southeast Asia Conference of 1950, alert, intelligent, at home in my private office, glancing over all dispatches, reading all letters, moving at will in and out of the Mansion House near the Presidential Palace, and meeting all the plenipotentiaries and the ambassadors of the countries struggling to uphold freedom in the Far East. I had big plans for both these bright young men.

One afternoon as I was preparing for an official trip to Washington, with Manuel scheduled to accompany me, I received two callers in my office in the Department of Foreign Affairs. One was from Central Intelligence and the other from the National Bureau of Investigation, the Filipino equivalent of the F.B.I. They spoke to me secretly and with great solemnity.

"General, do you know that you have two Communists in your Department of Foreign Affairs?"

They named Roberto and Manuel.

I was indignant. I sputtered denials—one young man had been with me in the United Nations, both at the Baguio Southeast Asia Conference!

Then their dossiers were shown to me. I read and had nothing more to say. I had regarded these young men as sons and had given them every opportunity, every responsibility and trust that would aid them in their advance. And they belonged on the side that was undermining freedom's last chance of survival in our country.

It was another Hiss case.

How I had been duped! I looked back over their records and remembered Roberto and his friendships and opinions along the way, recognizing, now that it was too late, the influences that had flattered and lured him into siding with the Communists. The agents were waiting to hear what I had to say, but I had no suggestions to make. There were no excuses to be made, neither for the two as plotters, nor for myself for having unwittingly aided them in their plans for the great betrayal. I could only shake my head stupidly, and say, "Do with them what must be done."

That was my first personal indication of what was going on all around us. The Reds were everywhere, at the next table, in the next room, at the desk next to mine. There was no time left in which to ask: How has this happened! How has this advanced so far!

We were too close to the Asian mainland to feel any sense of security. We knew what was going on there.

I went to the United States that year on a hurried trip to receive a Doctor of Laws degree from Harvard University, along with the then U.S. Secretary of State Dean Acheson. In my speech of acceptance I warned that the cold war in Asia was leading up to an explosion, possibly, I said, in Korea.

One week later North Korea attacked the South Koreans.

If you had asked me two years before, as many did, if the Philippines could ever turn Communist, I would have given a pitying and superior smile and answered proudly, "Never!" In fact, I gave that answer, many times. Turn Red, our Christian Land, that had been trained in democratic ideals and had fought to uphold those ideals from Corregidor to the hills in our farthest provinces? Never in a thousand years!

But it almost happened.

To find the explanation one had only to look at the fallen giant that was China. According to the Red communiques, the Chinese masses had rushed gladly into the embracing Soviet arms. This is always the Soviet story, and it is always based on the same Red lie. The Chinese had not embraced Communism. They did not regard the Soviet as their saviors. They had been starved, beaten, and betrayed into the Red net.

Not by the Reds! By brother Chinese!

I looked back to the China I had seen before the war. On that trip, circling through Southeast Asia, I had seen democracy in its last flickerings of life. It was not Communism that had won in China. It was loss of faith that lost China to Communism.

The Chinese had in Chiang Kai-shek a great leader, honest and sincere and a Christian. But like other leaders in other lands he had about him those who exploited him and who bartered China in exchange for wealth and luxury. China, too, had its overly rich, its grafters, its experts in corruption.

Before the war I had traveled the Burma Road. I had seen American materials landed in Rangoon, and by the time they reached their destination at the end of the road only one fifth remained. The rest had been lost along the way in the greasing of palms.

This had been struggling China, where a handful in power could speculate and enrich themselves and the common people were ignored, where nothing was done for the people, where their chance at life, and their way of living was never improved. The poor men of China lived as they had lived for centuries, fed by poverty, misery, hunger, and disease.

Then into China, as into other lands equally depressed, had come this new promise, this new hope that gave them the feeling they too might be regarded as human. Communism was a new power, if untried, and why fight for the old that had given nothing and taken all? Why fight to retain squalor and misery? Why fight to retain a government that had become meaningless, in which the people could hold no faith?

So reasoned China, and the poor tired soldier of China threw away his gun made in America and said: "Let the new order take over. I will fight no more."

Communism had usurped victory in China. It had not won. To the starvelings there the ideology of Marx was nothing compared to the fistful of rice that can keep a man alive for another day. Communism did not express

114

his longings. It was not his religion. His only thought was for change, any change that offered the last dim hope of staying alive.

"Change!" had been the last cry of China. "Any change will be better than this."

On that cry it had gone down.

That was the cry of the starving and it had been heard in Moscow. This was the echo—the thunder of China, falling.

Now in my own country I heard on every hand the demand for change. I heard the Kremlin propaganda quoted as gospel by those who did not know but who were ready to believe anything to escape present reality, and I saw that what had happened in China was taking place in my own country. The Red invaders were in our midst and preparing to take over.

Who was supporting them? Wherever one looked the signs pointed straight to Malacañan, to the very heart of our government in which the people had placed all their hopes, only to lose them.

What had happened in China was being repeated one year later in the Philippines.

It is important to stress again that what was undermining democracy in the Philippines was not fear of the Huks and belief in the Huk propaganda, but collapse of the people's faith in the government they had hoped for and fought for. Here was the independence they had wanted, and what did it mean to them! Nothing but greater poverty, and lowering suspicion. But on the other hand there were the Huks, and they could be understood. They at least did not hide their aims. Even as bandits, they were understandable. They were out to get while they could. But the Filipinos saw in the new government only another form of banditry that worked under cover of authority and that gave to the privileged few while pretending to be for the masses.

This was a return to the old days under Spain!

The Filipinos had revolted against Spain. They were revolting now. This was revolution—the peasant's refusal to till the land, the policeman's refusal to quell the Red disturbances, the soldier's refusal to try to subdue the Huks. Their attitude was the attitude the Chinese had taken at last toward the Red invasion. "What difference can it make to us? And either way, nothing can be worse. Any change will be better than this. . . ."

And all over the Islands this was heard, and people who had disapproved of the Huks and who were not active in the movement were now helping the Huks under the gathering volume of that cry. Our people had fought for change, and there was no change, save for the worse: graft and corruption they had not had before. They would not fight again. Men who had fought like tigers on Bataan and Corregidor and who were still in uniform, when out on foray under Presidential orders made token challenge by firing a few shots into the air against the Huks who, forewarned, were always elsewhere. The Huks, killers and sadists, were in power. They could excuse their worst crimes with their printed leaflets that pointed out crimes committed under the shadow of Malacañan: "See, the Government has done worse!"

And to these charges there were no answers to be made.

Here was the same deadly inertia that had betrayed

116

other countries to Communism, spreading among the people, sapping their last feeble protests—an inertia born of the conviction that their government was not worth saving.

It was in this crisis that casually and almost as if by chance the man appeared who was to save democracy and the Philippine Republic.

Truly, the times had found the man.

Chapter VIII

RAMÓN MAGSAYSAY is as little like a human prodigy as it is possible for a man to be. In this year of 1950, he was forty-three years old, and from a political point of view, he was virtually unknown. There was nothing outstanding about him, he was by no means cultured, he was not brilliant. His manners and his ways were those of the native Filipino. He did not smoke, gamble, or drink. He could speak in the native dialects which had been his as a child.

He is pure Malayan. His father was a Tagalog, his mother Ilocano. His name, Magsaysay, is from the Tagalog, and means "to tell a story."

He was born on August 31, 1907, at Iba in the granite hills of Zambales, the second of eight children of Exequiel Magsaysay and Perfecta del Fierro Magsaysay. The father taught carpentry in the school of their small town. This in itself was a step upward for a Filipino of the barrios and an illustration of that characteristic which the Filipino alone possesses among all the peoples of Asia: that urge to progress which imbues all levels of the Filipino people and which defies the age-old Asian concept that a son must not rise above the social level of his father.

118

The young Ramón lived the life of any simple lad of the barrios. He was trained in hard labor. His hard-working father wakened his sons at six every morning and when not in school they worked on the farm. The boy learned how to plow and how to swing a sledge in the smithy. He came to know and revere the land. From his parents he learned religion and honesty, the last to an almost painful degree. So honest was his father, that he was dismissed from the school for flunking the son of the superintendent of schools! This was when Ramón was ten. As a result the family were obliged to move to Castillejos, another village about thirty miles away. Ramón walked twenty-two kilometers a day to attend the high school at Zambales Academy in San Narciso, where he was graduated as salutatorian.

His later scholastic record was less outstanding. He would laugh years later, when his far-from-good school records were brought to light during a tense part of his career. He would always be a man of deeds, not words. He was to laugh also at his lack of training in social finesse, and to report gleefully after his first visit to Malacañan how dismayed he had been by the array of table silver, and how he had no idea which fork to use. But he attended school when he could, enrolling at the University of the Philippines at the age of twenty, starting with a liberal-arts course but soon switching to mechanical engineering; then he dropped out, and later worked his way through the José Rizal College, with a part-time job with a transportation company. He was graduated in 1932 with a degree of Bachelor of Science in Commerce.

His real interest at this time was cars. His father had

119

acquired an automobile while the boy was still at home, and Ramón had shown a natural aptitude for keeping it in running order. His father has said he took that car apart and put it together again every day.

Magsaysay was working for a bus concern one year after graduation when he married pretty Luz Banzon of Bataan province, the daughter of a well-to-do family also engaged in the passenger-bus business. Mrs. Magsaysay has said Ramón helped win her family's esteem with the excellent care he took of the family car.

By the time the Japanese attacked the Philippines, Ramón Magsaysay was well advanced in a steadily developing business career. He was branch manager of a transportation company, running a fleet of one hundred and fifty buses. His married life was happy. He was the father of two daughters and a son.

His public life may be said to have begun in war.

It is of no small significance that when war opened two courses to Magsaysay, he chose the direct but dangerous way. In those early days of the Japanese occupation, when General Homma's armies came thundering down on Manila with their antiquated motor transport, a man in Magsaysay's position, with a considerable amount of motor transport under his control and a great deal of mechanical "know-how," might have stayed on in Manila and gained greatly for himself both in security and in material wealth by joining the enemy, thereby following the example set by so many others who had far less to gain from the Japanese.

The way Magsaysay chose promised nothing but immediate danger to himself and incalculable hardship to a young family. It was the dedicated way of democracy.

He turned his fleet of cars over to the United States Army and enlisted as a volunteer with the Thirty-first Infantry Division. He fought until Bataan fell, then he helped organize the Western Luzon Guerrilla Forces, and headed ten thousand men. For three years he fought and starved in the Luzon hills with a Japanese price on his head.

In January, 1945, after United States troops invaded Luzon, Magsaysay's guerrillas secured the Zambales coast and made it possible for American soldiers to land in that area unopposed. Thousands of American lives were saved.

General MacArthur by this time had heard a great deal about the exploits of guerrilla leader Ramón Magsaysay. One month after the landings on the coast he appointed Magsaysay Military Governor of Zambales. One year later Magsaysay turned over the province, which he had administered with exemplary efficiency, to the Philippine Commonwealth Government and took off his uniform.

He did not return to his business career. The war had taught him he had the ability to lead. Philippine independence was only a few months away. He entered politics. In April, 1946, he was elected Representative of Zambales by the biggest majority in the history of that province.

In Manila he was one of one hundred and two Congressmen. I met him first when he was a member of a large group welcoming me home. I was impressed by his open frankness and friendly manner and by his reputation for absolute honesty, a trait that by this time had attracted

121

the attention of certain political writers. He was repeatedly mentioned in newspaper lists as one of the ten best Congressmen. He was re-elected in 1949, serving during both terms as chairman of the Committee on National Defense. As a former guerrilla officer he was greatly interested in the veteran's affairs, and was sent on a two-man mission to Washington to work for veterans' benefits. He stayed in Washington for several months and as a result of his efforts the Filipino veterans were included in some of the benefits.

Magsaysay learned a great deal in Washington. He liked the American way of life and made many friends. He also established good contacts in the Pentagon. Everyone seemed to like him.

By the fall of 1950, when the armed Communist uprising led by the Huks reached the stage where we could truly say, "This is revolution," sober conferences were held in Malacañan as to what could be done to save the Philippines. President Quirino, beset by dread of the violent spearheads thrusting from every direction against the duly constituted government, and heeding at last the growing clamor of the people for a change, looked hurriedly about for a man to accept the post of Secretary of National Defense, with a directive to put an end to the Huk menace.

The post was vacant because of a controversy. After Quirino admitted that the army could not stop the uprising, Defense Secretary Ruperto Kangleon had requested that certain weaknesses in the high command be replaced. Quirino had refused and Kangleon resigned in fury. Now a man was needed to take his place.

Many leaders and groups came forward with suggestions.

The members of Congress remembered Magsaysay's war record and honesty and recommended him. Senator Tomás Cabili went to the President to urge Magsaysay's appointment.

There is an American group in Manila, the Joint United States Military Assistance Group (known as the JUSMAG), which is assigned as a military mission to aid and advise the Philippine government on defense problems. Major General Leland Hobbs of the mission, who had been with General MacArthur in Japan and who, therefore, had an inside knowledge of the Magsaysay success in guerrilla warfare, also was among those who believed that Ramón Magsaysay should be put in charge of the anti-Huk offensive.

All these and many more saw possibilities in this newcomer to the political field; I am proud to say I was among them. Together they convinced President Quirino that Magsaysay was the ideal candidate.

Always eager for action, Magsaysay was most certain of all that he was the man for the job, so when the President sent for him to sound out his views, Magsaysay was ready with a plan to control the Huks. The President approved both the plan and the man, and he appointed Ramón Magsaysay, a man few people knew, as Secretary of National Defense.

Magsaysay accepted the portfolio and resigned from Congress. That was in September.

Then a tornado started.

He found the Philippine military organization in a state

bordering on demoralization. Conditions were deplorable in the Department of Defense and worse in the uniformed forces. The latter especially had been weakened by the almost complete infiltration of political influence and machination. Officers openly intrigued for promotion and plush assignments, and it was a slogan that merit had given way to "pull" in army circles. The enlisted men went about their duties in a lackadaisical manner that reflected the indifference of the higher echelons to the security problems threatening the nation. The army that had fought so courageously against Japan wasn't interested in fighting the newer enemy composed of Filipinos, misled and mainly ignorant, but fanatically convinced of the justice of their mission to overthrow the democratic government and supplant it with one based on the Soviet style.

By no stretch of the imagination can we conceive that there were traitor Communists or fellow travelers in the armed forces of the Philippines, or even in positions of influence. The real traitor in the army, as elsewhere, was national inertia. The service was riddled with the debilitating influence of favoritism and politics, and this was inevitably reflected in the "campaigns" conducted against the well-armed and dedicated followers of Taruc, Lava, Alejandrino, Capadocia, Balgos, and the other convert leaders to Communism. The constabulary having proved ineffectual, the job had been turned over to the army, which had proved equally futile, making no more effort than had the police to meet these dangerous groups at close combat. On the other hand, soldiers were helping themselves to private property, such as cattle, chickens, and food, under the guise of conducting the "anti-Huk campaign," while the campaign itself had deteriorated into a few shots fired into the jungle, here and there and now and then.

This was all that was being done to protect the Philippines against a revolutionary movement that threatened to take over the government any day and any hour. No wonder the people had lost faith in their once-respected army, which had failed them, along with everything else they had trusted!

Magsaysay got right to work on a twenty-four-hours-a-day job. He was no office man. His swivel chair stood empty; he was out in the field. First he had to make the army believe in itself and imbue it with respect for this vital offensive, then the people had to be made to respect and trust in the army again and stop tolerating and protecting the Huks which they had come to believe was the lesser of two evils. This meant readjusting all around: the soldiers to the honor code and the spirit of service, and the people to regarding the soldiers as their friends and protectors, rather than their oppressors.

He began with a reorganization of the army that set the "deadwood" high brass shaking in their boots. A government shakedown placed the ineffective constabulary directly under the armed forces, and then shrank it down in size to about seven thousand officers and men. The remainder were absorbed into the army. The campaign for the restoration of peace and order was transferred directly to the armed forces under the direction of Magsaysay.

As systematically as once he had stripped down recalcitrant cars to discover their troubles, this ex-garage mechanic proceeded to strip down the newly reorganized army and put it together again in working order. First, he took the armed forces out of politics. He cleaned out the "deadwood" by rooting out all the incompetents who had won their stripes through favoritism. He promoted those officers who were actually making an effort to fight the Huks (he could not demote those who didn't, though he longed to), and he went on sweeping aside army brass in a way that caused panic in the upper echelons. He was referred to by certain officers as "That ignorant guerrilla."

A committee of generals protested his wholesale army shifts. "You are kicking out too many officers and men. You will demoralize the army!" To which he replied: "I don't care. If they are bad I will demoralize them some more." He ferreted out those officers who, although not out-and-out Communists, were serving as liaison links with the dissident forces and who had been sending secret warnings to the Huks when the army was about to launch one of its halfhearted attacks.

This snipped the lifeline between the army and the Huks. But the people remained to be convinced of the army's sincerity. They still had ways of getting information to the Huks, and means for keeping them subsidized.

It was going to be a big fight, and Magsaysay needed money to carry it through. We had no money in the Philippines. I used to look out over Manila Bay and estimate how much of our good silver and gold lay under its waters, tossed overboard in our attempt to help balance the scales for democracy. We needed it now as badly as we had needed it in the days when we were fighting Japan.

Magsaysay asked President Quirino to send me, as Secretary of Foreign Affairs, to Washington to ask for money, and to arouse America to the fact that the cancer of Communism was eating away the Philippines' last chance of survival as a democratic nation.

In Washington I laid our plans before General George Marshall, Secretary of Defense, and he wired General Hobbs, who flew from Manila to Washington to back up my arguments. If we waited for a Congressional appropriation it would be too late; the momentum of our offensive against the Huks would be lost.

General Marshall consulted the Chiefs of Staff, the National Security Council, and President Truman, and ten million dollars was taken from the Defense Department and given to Magsaysay to use as he saw fit.

The United States Government knew that every penny of that money would be honestly spent.

It was given us, in this year 1950, by the United States to help us fight the new enemy, Communism, in the Philippines, and to counter the attacks against "United States imperialism" by Soviet propaganda on the Far Eastern front.

Once more, Filipinos and Americans were fighting together. There was no glory in this defense on the Asian battle line. It was a grubby struggle to root out an octopus ideology that had fastened itself on the minds of millions.

Just the same, it was war, and I do not suppose the average American, tending his garden after work hours, knew of the all-out struggle his country was subsidizing in the Philippines to protect his right to tend his bit of ground.

The ten million dollars sparked the all-out offensive against the Huks; nevertheless, our fight against Communism was costing the Filipinos one-third of our national government spending. This was a cruel penalty leveled by Communism against a struggling and impoverished young nation. The Huks were making it almost impossible for the Philippines to survive as a republic, and only a man with the energy and honesty of Ramón Magsaysay was capable of saving the Philippines at this late hour.

With a rebuilt and revitalized army of forty thousand troops, Magsaysay went out after the Huks in the same violent fashion he had gone after the Japanese, and with an energy and determination that surpassed their own. In olive drab, and with only four hours sleep a night, he was in action everywhere and anywhere, stirring up trouble for the enemy or for the recalcitrant in his own forces wherever he appeared.

To make certain that his army reforms were carried out, Magsaysay made personal post inspections, ducking about in surprise visits from one army outpost to another in a C-47 or army car, or even by carabao cart in hills where no car could go. At one post Magsaysay and his aide surprised a sleepy sergeant who had been left alone to guard an ammunition and supply dump. They detained the man and took him before the commandant.

"We might have been Huks," Magsaysay pointed out, removing the officer then and there and relieving him of his command.

He was as quick to praise. On the battlefield, there on the spot, he gave out promotions and decorations. The soldiers began to realize this was a new deal, that merit would be recognized. Also, this new leader was one of their own kind. He spoke to them in their own tongues. In

English or native dialects, he could make himself understood in pungent and direct prose. His bravery was, of course, legendary; now he led many a sortie into the jungle, showing an utter disregard for his own safety, and exposing himself to the enemy as fearlessly as he had to the Japanese. With his guerrilla knowledge he was able to ferret out the Huks' jungle hideouts and lead the way. He could counter every Huk guerrilla tactic with better guerrilla tactics, and he struck swiftly and hard at the Huk concentrations with small but well-armed mobile units, giving the rebels no time to rest, reorganize, and replenish their stocks of arms and provisions.

Actually, this was the sort of life he loved. This was the kind of war he understood. He was no armchair general. He had fought and suffered as a guerrilla, and he knew how the guerrillas were living and how they fought.

He also knew the men he was leading. He was one of them. Whenever trouble started he was with them, out in the hills and jungles, leading the way, eating, bivouacking, talking with the men. He imbued them—or rather re-imbued them, for many of them had fought against the Japanese in the three-and-a-half years of resistance—with the will to attack, to attack, and always to attack.

There were no more of the desultory "demonstrations" and token attacks—the firing of a few aimless rounds of artillery—which had permitted the Huk movement to exist and grow.

Officers and men had formed the habit of returning from such forays with impressive accounts of the large numbers of Huks left dead on the field. We had a saying in the Philippines that if only half the number of Huks had been killed that the army laid claim to having killed, only a very small proportion of the Filipino population would be left alive!

Magsaysay arrested this fiction by providing his commanding officers with cameras and ordering them to take photographs of the dead Communists killed in action, as direct proof that they were really dead.

He posted awards for Huks dead or alive, demanding proof of identity, and persuaded President Quirino to suspend the writ of habeas corpus for all prisoners reported to be Huks. He put a price of one hundred thousand pesos on Luis Taruc's head, and that "Huk supremo" at once ducked under cover in the hills where, surrounded by faithful Communists and protected by the citizenry, he continued to be a thorn in the government's side long after other Huk leaders had been captured or slain.

Every soldier fighting on the side of democracy was like a son to Magsaysay. He watched over his men and listened to their stories. Every enlisted man who killed a Huk received from him a personal letter of commendation and a one-stripe promotion.

His very presence among the men was helping to whip the army into an efficient fighting machine. Morale soared. The men were taking pride in being part of the Philippine Army, in their uniforms and arms and bearing—a pride that had been lost since the war.

They loved him, even when he curtailed certain privileges they had been led to regard as a soldier's prerogative. It had been their privilege to help themselves freely to eggs and chickens and other farm produce to supplement army chow, and without the consent of the owners.

Magsaysay heard of many such misdeeds in many villages, and sent for the complainants. If such charges were proved the miscreants were punished in the presence of the villagers.

This made a great impression on the people who had been complaining that the army was no better than the Huks.

The army continued to gain in integrity and determination, and the people who had lost faith in their armed forces and the government it represented began to experience a revival of faith. People began citing this new integrity and saying, "Here is justice!" which was a way of saying, "Here is a changing government in which we may be able to believe again."

And just as in proportion to the rise of graft and corruption in the government, Communism had grown, so now in proportion to the revival of justice the people began gradually to lessen their support of the Huks.

It was Magsaysay's first impulse to wipe out all the enemy, down to the last man. Even though they were Filipinos, they were Moscow-inspired and, hence, traitors, and he wanted to see every Communist in the Philippines exterminated, if necessary, with a violence to match their own.

The tactics used against the Huks were not always orthodox. They could not be. The Huks were not fighting along the accepted conventional lines. They were fighting guerrilla warfare outside the lines of military law, and they were not bound by any of the legal, constitutional, and moral laws which handicapped the army. To keep the subjugated areas under control the Huks were committing more criminal acts than ever—extortion, kidnapping torture, and always murder. The army could not retaliate in kind. On the other hand, every Huk captured clamored with full knowledge of the legal and constitutional code for his "rights," which, in all honor, had to be given him. So the democratic side was handicapped in many ways by the very force of its democracy; a handicap that has not been missing in history from countries other than our own.

Freedom always gives an unfair advantage to those who fight against freedom. That is its greatest handicap, and its greatest power.

Despite this disadvantage, the anti-Huk campaign was carried on in full force in the affected areas, which were principally in the islands of Luzon and Panay. The core of the Red infection was in the central plains of Luzon, where the province of Pampanga, with its heavy burden of absentee landlordism, had offered the greatest breeding areas to the Communist cause. Half of the Philippines' twenty-one million people are concentrated on the island of Luzon.

The Huks had organized Central Luzon into ten regional, and one city, commands. Magsaysay and his advisors worked out a plan whereby the population of the endangered areas were to be protected by garrisons, then the enemy regional commands were to be attacked one by one.

The people, who were learning to trust in the government again, responded to this plan by flocking back to the barrios and homes from which they had been driven by the Huks, to take up their lives again under the protection of the army garrisons. There was a disadvantage to this plan that made itself apparent almost at once. So many of the people flocked for protection back into the barrios and towns, and so many soldiers were required to protect them, that only a greatly reduced number of troops were left to carry on the offensive against the Huks. Also it was clear that a great many Huks were mixing freely with the civilians, hearing everything that was being planned and learning about the army's proposed attacks before they were made. The enemy was as elusive and hard to catch as before. Sorties were sent out to encampments from which all the Huks had vanished as if by magic. The troops were wild for action now, but where could action be found!

The people were still shielding the enemy within, in mortal fear of that enemy. The Huks had demonstrated how cruel they could be. It is not easy to persuade frightened people to talk.

The Huks had their carefully organized intelligence service, run by terror. The democratic side had none, and never was one more needed and for a better cause. But the organization of such a service would require funds to subsidize information, so the anti-Huk campaign was threatened at its very start. A curious incident routed it into the right way.

On Magsaysay's first day in office as Defense Secretary he received a message from a man he did not know, asking him to come alone and unarmed to a midnight rendezvous in a nipa hut in one of the slum sections of Manila. Magsaysay made inquiries and was told that the man was a well-known Huk and he was strongly advised not to take the risk. But there was a certain cops-and-robbers appeal in the challenge for Magsaysay, and at midnight he set out alone and without a gun, following his instincts down some of the darkest and loneliest alleys in the city to keep the secret tryst.

For several hours he sat talking with the Huk in the palm-frond hut. The man was nervous and seemed to be expecting others; Magsaysay had no illusions as to what they were. But the expected visitors did not arrive and Magsaysay took advantage of the time to argue and plead with the Huk the dangers of the Red side and the triumph that would come with siding with democracy.

He made a strong impression on the Huk, as he had with so many others; as he would with so many more. When he left, the Huk asked if he would come again, alone.

Several times, alone, unarmed, at midnight, Magsaysay visited the hut in the slums and on each visit he won the trust of the Huk a little more. Once he asked Magsaysay to give him money. He was poor; he wanted to buy a car. Without a word of rebuke, Magsaysay gave him the money.

He had made a convert and a friend. The Huk told him that on that first midnight a jeepload of Huk triggermen had been due to arrive at the nipa hut and kill Magsaysay. He had served as decoy. It had been carefully planned. Something had gone wrong, and the Huks did not appear.

Then, thoroughly impressed by Magsaysay's courage and honesty, he exposed to him the details of the Philippine Communist Party's Politburo which had set up its headquarters in the very heart of Manila and was openly threatening to seize the capital. Everyone knew that the top Huk members, the most dangerous of the enemy, were living secretly in the city, but no one knew who they were or where they were hiding.

Magsaysay's Huk friend told him to assign men to follow a twelve-year-old girl. Under the guise of a vendor of meats and vegetables she went boldly through the streets at regular hours, leaving food and secret messages with the Huk leaders in hiding.

The girl was followed and the lairs of the Huk leaders located and surrounded. As a result the twelve top members of the Communist Politburo were captured, tried, convicted, and sentenced to imprisonment or death. Those who escaped fled to the hills. All the members were eventually captured with the exception of one who was later killed in battle with an army unit that had been sent to take him dead or alive.

The fall of the Politburo exposed the Communist plans to the last detail. It was Magsaysay's first victory over the enemy, and it produced definite results. Not only were other Huks persuaded to talk, but the new channels of information opened called for a rapid shift in plans. Up to this time the directive had been to exterminate the entire enemy force. But the first Huk won over by Magsaysay to the democratic side was convincing proof that the Huks need not be regarded as a total loss to democracy. Magsaysay became certain that many could be salvaged.

So the plan was changed from all-out destruction of the enemy to the destruction of enemy leadership. The new directive called for larger striking forces and a relentless drive against the enemy groups, the disrupting of enemy communications, sources of information and supplies and the destruction of their hiding places, and the intensification of military intelligence and psychological warfare.

The unconventional Huks were being attacked along unconventional lines.

Magsaysay's methods were as bold as they were unorthodox. The Huks had infiltrated; our men counterinfiltrated. The Huks had spy schools in the hills. Magsaysay organized spy schools. The Huks wore many disguises, such as women's clothing. Our soldiers on occasion dressed as women.

A great deal of the action against the Huks followed the conventional lines of warfare, but there were methods used in scouting, patrol, and attack which were guerrilla ways, learned in a tough school by guerrilla-leader Magsaysay. An increasing amount was done with the full understanding and cooperation of the citizens, who gained in courage as their trust in the army was renewed. As a result, barrios and towns were screened for spies with gratifying results, and ambush parties were sent out to cover enemy trails on tips reported by the growing intelligence. Magsaysay was fighting the Huks with their own best weapons by infiltrating the Huk forces with his own agents, winning the trust of the people who had been shielding them, making friends with the families of Huks, and promising them security from the Huks if they refused to protect and provide for them any more.

Then to every Huk who surrendered he pledged amnesty, restored citizenship, and a job; in other words, a new chance at a new life.

Huks began surrendering. Magsaysay talked to them, man to man. They became his friends.

He made friends of other Huks who had been captured. Some of these he persuaded to rejoin their outfits and serve as his secret agents inside the Red lines. Others he organized into anti-Huk brigades who fought as staunchly against their former allies as they had fought beside them. Not one of these men ever let Magsaysay down.

With a commando force made up entirely of ex-Huks he invaded the mountain sanctuaries of Huk Command Number Six on the Island of Panay, which was under the command of the high-ranking Red leader, Guillermo Capadocia. The enemy was powerfully entrenched in these hills where they had set up a Soviet stronghold and had even built so-called Stalin Universities and other Soviet training schools. Our forces captured and killed Capadocia and scattered his commune into small ineffectual bands that were forced to skulk like animals in the hills.

Taruc, too, was in hiding, under the protection of a shrinking number of followers. Taruc still was a power to reckon with and was feared. Otherwise the Red forces were dwindling rapidly. Lava, who had trained Taruc, was dead.

The Huks retaliated against the Magsaysay success by raiding his home town. After the men were killed every woman and child the Huks could lay their hands upon became the bloody victim of massacre. Magsaysay was terribly aroused.

Even so, he could be temperate. When one of the Huks who had taken part in the atrocity was captured, Magsaysay might understandably have had him shot as "trying to

137

escape." But he sent for the man and they talked together for a long time. Finally he let him go with the encouraging words, "I think you can become a good citizen and I'm going to give you a chance to prove it."

All that Magsaysay was doing was winning back the tried hearts of a proud people who had thought themselves betrayed. Magsaysay had implicit faith in the people. "We can't win this war without them," he often said.

He was winning friends on every side, and at the same time, in proof of his high success, the man Magsaysay was making enemies. Do not think all he was doing met with approval in all circles! His wiping out of the weak army brass and his unconcern for the rights of "pull" and nepotism and power-in-office were interfering with certain well-made plans. Some of the powerfully entrenched were watching with growing dismay the sweeping tactics of this unpolished diamond from the barrios. Some of the "get-rich-quick lads" were interrupted in their getting, and they rightly laid the blame on the new Minister of Defense whose defensive tactics were uncovering some very strange situations. There were those who were openly jealous and disturbed by his quick rise to power. There were those who did not care which party got in so long as their own pockets were well lined, and since Magsaysay's democratic campaign was interfering with their quick-profits campaign, they found it easy to blame and to hate Magsaysay.

Had he been willing to pull his punches in these crucial years of 1950-1951, a great deal of misbegotten wealth might have found its way into the pockets of Magsaysay's olive drabs. We know of the many tempting offers made him under the guise of proffered "gifts." Chinese visas, campaign donations, booty from the depleted treasury chest of a looted nation—all might have been his.

His sense of honesty remained adamant. He once said that if his own father broke the law he would put him in jail.

One evening he strode into Malacañan and interrupted a state dinner with a request to speak at once to President Quirino. He had with him a trembling officer and two large bags containing one hundred and fifty thousand pesos. The officer had uncovered a secret ammunition cache and been advised to forget it, and to aid his lapse in memory he had been offered the bribe. The officer had taken the money and brought it to Magsaysay, who wanted him praised and rewarded on the spot.

Poor President Quirino! He had to commend the officer and promote him from captain to major, between courses.

Justice had returned to the Philippines, tempered with Christian mercy.

Justice which comes straight from the heart, even the simplest can understand.

Within a few months after the little-known Ramón Magsaysay had become head of defense in the Philippines, he had won more than the unswerving loyalty of the armed forces. He had behind him the faith and the almost solid support of the Filipino people.

It was the start of the turning back to democracy.

Chapter IX

WITHIN a year Magsaysay had reduced the Huk rebellion from a major national threat to a movement of insignificant proportions; more of a nuisance than a real menace to the security and stability of the Philippine Republic. The Huks continued to retreat, to yield, to break up.

Again one could walk in the streets of Manila and drive through the roads of Luzon without fear.

The armed forces still had enough to keep them occupied. Along with the job of administering the new farm movement, which I will later describe in detail, the troops were kept busy collecting loose firearms, supervising civilian guards, screening town officials for Huk influence, training and aiding the constabulary, guarding the crops and stock of the farmers from any stray Huks, and supervising elections.

The election assignment was due directly to Magsaysay. The "dirty election" of 1949 had done incalculable harm to national morale and turned thousands of citizens pro-Huk who had never before harbored any Communist ideas.

Now the election of 1951 was coming up and the rallying cry of the politicos-in-power was once again, "Bullets instead of ballots." Again the goons were hired and guns oiled to keep the people away from the polls.

The Presidency was not at stake this year, but control of the Senate was the issue. The fight would be bitter; for the "dirty election" was fresh in all minds, and on every side one heard people saying ominously that a repeat version of the terrorism of 1949 would bring on revolution. The people had found voice again and the popular clamor grew until President Quirino was obliged to promise to prevent intimidation. Magsaysay was the natural choice to be put in charge of the election.

Magsaysay had an announcement ready. This election, he promised, would be known as the "clean election." It would be an erasure of the blot from 1949.

He knew, when he made that promise, that he was risking his political future. His challenge to the hirelings was a direct challenge to the powers who hired them, and among these, some were those in power who were steeped in graft and spoils and would disapprove of any change. In certain instances he was defying the very ones who had helped him to his present position of power. But his loyalty went beyond them to the people who were joining in the fight to preserve democracy and were entitled to every right democracy had to give.

He knew he was expressing the will of the people when he promised the "clean election." Then, to guarantee its cleanliness he ordered out his troops.

He called out other surprise defenders along with the soldiers. He drew on the manpower of the students and the educators. Teachers served as polling clerks without pay. ROTC cadets served as election guards. Soldiers protected the ballot boxes. Other soldiers guarded the voters to and from their homes, forestalling as much as possible the intimidation and bloodshed that had made the 1949 election a world-wide scandal.

The senatorial election was not entirely free of bloodshed. Most of the fighting took place before the election was held. Before the polls were opened ninety-six people were dead, among them several of the candidates for election, and more than a hundred had been kidnapped. But these atrocities did not go unpunished as before. In one town where a pre-election killing occurred, Magsaysay ordered the entire police force arrested and charged with murder. In another town a candidate was kidnapped; Magsaysay jailed the mayor.

As a result, election day, when it arrived, was almost an anticlimax. The hired gangsters had turned back their guns to their politico bosses and nearly all had disappeared. Four million Filipinos made their way in almost complete safety to the polling places and on a mighty wave of enthusiasm voted the anti-Quirino candidates into all the contested seats and control of the Senate.

Out of these four million, twenty-one lost their lives on the day of the "clean election." In the "dirty election" many hundreds had been killed.

The "clean election" turned the full force of public attention on Magsaysay. People began saying, "Here is a man who knows how to get things done! Here is a leader. . . ."

These comments did not go unheard in the upper echelons of those in power. Then Magsaysay really headed for a stone wall of opposition and resentment with his EDCOR Project, the movement to return the Huks to the land without reprisal.

This project in a way came out of the human laboratories he had established in Manila in the effort to understand the Huk problem in its entirety, not as a military problem alone, but as a human one.

These bureaus were started shortly after he had become Secretary of Defense and had won the first Huks to the democratic side simply by talking with them and finding out why they had turned Huks, and how they could be turned away from Communism and back to democracy.

Dead, the Huks presented no problem. Alive, they had answers to give, and he wanted to hear what they were. He was *willing* to hear.

Always, even in his relatively subordinate capacity of a minister of the cabinet, Magsaysay had in mind the fact that these Huks he was fighting were his own people— misguided, hostile to all his principles, yet his own. In a national crisis he had been forced to use the mailed fist, but now the crisis was ebbing and there was time to don the velvet glove. These wholesale killings were against his conscience and against the nation's; besides, he was becoming more and more convinced that bullets were not the answer. The government was proving it could destroy all its enemies, but was it not more politic, as well as Christian, to give those enemies a chance to redeem themselves in normal society?

So the warfare with guns and guerrilla tactics changed wherever possible to psychological warfare, with ideas that went deeper than bullets, aimed directly at the Huks and indirectly at the whole Filipino nation.

The arsenals of the new attack were the offices of the human-relations bureau in Manila, where kindness and understanding were the ammunition issued, and a friendly word and a proffered cigarette were found to carry as potent a power as a tommy gun aimed at the human heart.

In these bureaus army officers trained in interrogation questioned the Huk prisoners and persuaded them to speak. There was no brain-washing, no cross-examination, no threats or force. Prisoner and officer sat down together and the prisoner was permitted to air his grievances without fear.

As a rule the captive Huks were eager to talk. They were burning to bring out the old grievances that had driven them into the hills.

The explanations they gave were simple, but they are the stories of human beings, and they must be studied by those who would know how a democratic people can be turned to Communism.

One by one the same reasons came from the embittered ones: Because they had not found the democratic justice and freedom they had hoped and fought for during the long war against the Japanese. Because they had been given reason to distrust men who to them represented the government.

Magsaysay retold their stories in turn in Cabinet meetings in explanation of the way Communists are made. He told of the Filipino who deserted his village to fight in the hills with the Huks because of the justice of the peace who had refused to grant justice. In this man's case, his daughter had been employed as a servant in the household of the mayor. The girl was made pregnant and the father believed that the mayor was guilty. He went with his oldest son to the mayor's house to bring his daughter home, but the mayor refused to let her go, and when father and son protested, the mayor sent for the justice of the peace who took them both off to jail. At the end of the week they were released only to learn that the daughter was dead. They were told she had committed suicide. They were also ordered to get out of town. They did. They joined the Huks in the hills, not because the Communist ideology meant anything to them, but because their own authorities had failed them.

The Huks had their ears to the ground. They knew how to handle such cases.

They learned of them when they came into the barrios by night to see their families and get supplies. A committee would call on the troubled man. "Join us," they would urge, "and we will get justice for you. You can get it in no other way under this crooked government."

So a crude justice would be performed, and from that time on the avenged one was an outlaw. He was a Communist. A Huk. Ideology had had nothing to do with bringing him into the Red fold.

Here is a form of injustice that was cited many times: The poor tao—Juan de la Cruz as we call the John Doe of the Philippines—has as a rule no *padrino*, no sponsor to explain matters to him and for him. He is usually a poor countryman with scant knowledge and great fear of the Government. He may have a small favor to ask of that

Government; his children, perhaps, are ill. The village herb doctor has said they are very ill. The tao walks a long distance from the farm to the town and the Government halls are large and frightening, and he feels very much alone speaking his humble request to the first man he sees behind a desk. The man, some minor official, often unscrupulous, looks down his nose at this barefooted suppliant and demands "payment" in advance. The poor tao does not know this is an unnecessary and illegal tip. He digs into his ragged pocket, unties his rag of handkerchief, and turns the sum over without suspicion, only to be sent from desk to desk, from office to office, perhaps from building to building, where other unscrupulous minor officials in turn demand tribute from the pitiful sum he has brought along.

He finds himself at last standing with trembling legs in the doorway of the dispensary in the City Hall. Another man glares at him over a desk. "What do you want?" He explains once more that his children are sick. The next question shocks him. "How much money have you?" He gives the last of the peso, the one hundred centavos he had tied into the handkerchief before leaving home, and says anxiously, "I have no more." The "official," who is often only the receptionist, may take it with sarcastic grumbling, then ask contemptuously, "What is wrong with your children?"

Now to the Filipino of the poorer levels there are only three illnesses—fever, a stomach trouble, and skin disease. The poor tao mutters that his children have fever. The official knows that this man comes from a malaria belt, so he hands him a bottle of quinine pills and waves him away. The man trudges home and gives his children the quinine; no one has prepared him for the chills which follow. He concludes his children have been poisoned and by his own Government, and he goes back a thousand years, back to the primitive, and sends for the herb doctor, who can always say that a child has been bewitched when it dies.

He has no money left with which to bury this child and he sits grieving and miserable in his hut that night beside his dead. And men come. They are Huks. They understand. They, too, have known bitterness. And they tell him, "It is the Government that has done this to you."

He knows the Government does not pay for funerals. But the Huks have money. They will see that his child has a decent burial. And after this has been done he learns that now he, too, is a Huk, not a fighter in the hills, for he cannot leave his family, but a Huk of the town, where he will gather information for the Huk groups and help to collect food for them.

The tao would tell this story in the bureaus with hopelessness and remembered bitterness, and say, "I needed help and was not given help. But the Huks knew and came to my aid."

The petty grafters who betrayed their government when they betrayed this humble father were guiltier than the Huks, for they were placed in what should have been positions of trust. They failed the tao and themselves when they failed democracy. These are the men who should wear the Communist brand!

147

It was clear that many of the Huks were criminals who had been made so by injustice. Some had avenged harm done to their wives and children. Many had taken action for injustices perpetrated against themselves by rich and heartless landlords.

In the remote barrios of the Philippines, feudal rights are as strong as they were in Spanish days. One Huk who had been a respectable tenant farmer told of his daughter, engaged to be married, who was violated by the owner of their land. When the father protested he was ordered off the land which he and his people had farmed for generations. He told the young man his daughter had been about to marry, and together they waylaid the landlord and killed him. Now they were both murderers and where could they go into hiding save into the hills with the Huks?

What had Soviet ideology to do with their conversion to Communism!

It became apparent that the majority of the Huk complaints came out of injustices concerning the land.

Our land laws in the Philippines came down to us from Spanish times. Great areas of farming land are owned by absentee landlords who farm them out to generations of tenant farmers and accept the yield of their crops in return. Also due to these ancient grants the authenticity of land titles is uncertain, so that a poor tao can farm his bit of land for generations and never be sure it is his.

For example, one Huk told of buying and clearing a patch of jungle and making it into good rice land after years of back-breaking labor. He cut the trees and pulled the stumps and planted the shoots and watched them grow. He built a nipa hut for his family with his own hands. He did not know that his land title was worthless and that a wealthy man in a nearby town was the actual owner of his farm. But the rich man knew, and when the rice was ready to reap he claimed the land and the house and the crop, and the farmer was turned out with his family to wander the roads. Robbed of the land he had paid and toiled for and the crops he had sown, homeless and embittered, where could he turn now but to the Huks? So another convert to Communism had joined the ranks.

It was learned that thousands of Huks had once been tenant farmers who might have toiled from boyhood to the end of their lives on land they could never own, farming the bits of land their fathers before them had rented and farmed, and struggling without hope to pay off the debts acquired by those fathers generations before. A rich landlord had allotted a bit of land to the man's grandfather, and had kindly thrown in a carabao and a plow; the grandfather had understood he could pay for this loan as the crops ripened. Now, a hundred years later, a man might gather three sacks of rice from that land, and carry it before his landlord, who would claim two. When the tenant farmer complained he could not feed his family on one sackful, and wanted to know why his year's work was so poorly rewarded, he was told the interest on the ancient loan was increasing and not decreasing with the years. Then he would return to his nipa hut knowing the debt could never be paid, that his family would never have

149

enough to eat, and that no matter how long or how hard he labored, the land, and the fruits of that land, could never be his.

What was this but slavery!

And the Huks who heard of his bitterness and came to his house by night agreed that this was indeed slavery, and that a man was a fool to work for another when he might live the free life in the hills. . . . Join the Huks, and some day all the land would be theirs!

An avalanche of such pent-up injustices kept pouring across the desks of the human-relations bureaus. The Huks had so many stories to relate, and all were heard. Injustices had driven men from the farms into the Huk-ridden hills, and others had fled the city for like reasons. In Manila, at this time, a workingman had to work hard to earn a dollar a day with which to buy food for his family—food that cost three times as much as it would in New York! The Filipino income per capita was under two hundred dollars per year, which was less than ten per cent of that in the United States.

Added grist for the Communist mill were the promises made and broken by the Filipino government itself. The Quirino administration had promised to enforce the minimum wage and initiate land reform. The United States had pledged more aid to the Philippines provided these reforms were made, and had even given us an advance on the promised sum. But nothing had been done about starting the reforms, and no one knew where the money had been spent.

All this was fodder for the Communist propagandists,

and what could be said by way of denial when the lack of concern around Malacañan was apparent to all!

People who have been deprived of land, food, justice, hope and pride, medical care for their families, education for their children, can at last hope only for change. When there is no change, they are prey for the Communist propagandists.

This was true in the Philippines. It is always true everywhere.

As a result of the studies made in the human-relations bureaus, Magsaysay came to believe that land was a fundamental power in solving the problem of Communism; that many Huks were not Communists by conviction: they were farmers who could no longer make a living on the land tenure, or who had never been permitted to own their land, or who had worked in the hopeless attempt to rid the land of debt and own it, or who had owned land and lost it through debt, or who had it taken from them by unjust means.

Here was something he could understand.

He himself was a man of the people, which is to say, of the land. He knew that love for the land. He realized why these men were fighting: for a place of their own! This had been the basic drive behind the threatened revolution.

He knew then that Communism could never be defeated with guns.

Acting on this conviction, Magsaysay brought into being a new approach to the Huk problem. He struck at the very heart of the evil that made the Huks possible when

151

he launched the project EDCOR—the army-backed Economic Development Corps whose purpose was to provide "land for the landless."

This was a direct counterattack to the Communist claim that the Huks were "agrarian reformers."

On his travels in the south, Magsaysay had seen great tracts of wasteland lying unclaimed on the underpopulated island of Mindanao. Now he urged the development of the Mindanao resettlement program. He wheedled large tracts of land on the southern island, and certain promises, out of President Quirino. Then he began his campaign to rehabilitate the Huks.

Word was broadcast to the Huks that to all who surrendered and showed a sincere desire to lead a peaceful life the government would give transportation for themselves and their families and such possessions as they could carry, as well as seeds, farm equipment, stock, a government-built cottage, and twenty-five acres of virgin soil on the island of Mindanao. This land they themselves could break and tend, to be theirs and their children's in perpetuity.

A miracle was worked.

The Huks began pouring into the garrisons by the hundreds to lay down their arms. Men who had been living in the hills like hunted animals, robbing and pillaging to eat, heard over the makeshift radios of the chance to live, without fear, with one's family again, to walk without fear into a town, to wake and sleep without fear of arrest, imprisonment, or death, and most of all, to be a landowner: Who would not surrender on such terms!

To those who capitulated it was explained that while the Republic was fully capable of stamping out the last enemy in its midst, it preferred taking the Christian way, and therefore all who were willing to live on working terms with the government could expect all the cooperation and aid the government could give.

With some of these who surrendered, Magsaysay conducted a daring experiment. He handed them back their guns and sent them on commando raids to bring in more Huks. Of the others, hundreds were transported south and established on the new land settlement at Mindanao.

There had been other Filipino land resettlement programs in the past. They had been left in the hands of the politicians. The moving of large groups of farm families from the crowded, Communist-breeding regions of Central Luzon to the untapped regions of Mindanao had been an administration project for some time. But in keeping with the usual inertia of the administration to the people's needs, little had come of it but complications and added discontent. The LASEDECO (Land Settlement and Development Corporation, a government project) was inept, inefficient, and in many ways subservient to vested interests far different from the needy displaced farmers. As a result groups of migrants were dumped on vacant land and left there, with no provision made to enable them to make a living or even to live. Somehow vast areas of rich land found their way into the hands of absentee landlords with the "right connections."

The unhealthy pattern of Central Luzon had been repeated in the "promised land" of Mindanao.

Actually, the new project was not a job for the army,

but Magsaysay did not hesitate to take it over. His role as Secretary of Defense was purely military, but since the politicians had failed, he would see what his soldiers could do. Magsaysay's EDCOR camps, established and managed under army supervision and his personal control, took charge of the former Huks and their families as they arrived on the big island. The newcomers' lands were allotted to them under army supervision. Then, recalling the false titles that had lost so many their land in the past, Magsaysay saw to it that the land registry office shortened its red tape and gave the tiller of the land his title free and clear within a reasonable time. Formerly, it had taken a title many years, often ten or fifteen, to go through the registry office. A Filipino could work a farm all that time and not be certain it was his own.

Now a land title could be cleared within two years. This was a radical improvement.

Magsaysay was as active in resettling the Huks as he had been in fighting them. If short cuts had to be taken, he took them. He once wanted to buy some war-surplus Quonset huts to use as schoolhouses, but the politician-profiteer-owner was holding them for an inflationary price. Magsaysay collected some of his former guerrillas, raided the Quonset dump, and made off with one hundred and forty huts. Later he paid the owner what Magsaysay knew he had paid for the huts in the first place—twenty-five cents for each building.

The Mindanao settlement proved a successful venture in land reform. It showed that such reform was vital to Philippine security. As word of its success spread through the outposts of the Huk command, Huks began pouring by the thousands into the garrisoned towns to offer their arms in exchange for the new and law-abiding life at Mindanao.

EDCOR has, literally, given the chance at new living to thousands of Huks who were willing to resume a life of peace and usefulness within the law, and who are to-day reaping bountiful harvests on their own farms which are for many the realization of the dreams of a lifetime.

The Philippines is fortunate in possessing large empty tracts of fertile land which are being portioned out among more and more land-hungry people, including many former Huks. The EDCOR project figures in a report of United Nations experts on community development who toured South and Southeast Asia last year. It is the most successful project in the Philippines today.

Magsaysay had been right. The simple art of understanding had proved more powerful than bullets in conquering the Huks.

As he said in a speech before the State Department in Washington: "We have to destroy the raw materials of the Communists, in other words, give land to the landless. The alternative is to use more ammunition to kill more Huks. I prefer to convert them."

One American official said after hearing that speech that Magsaysay had given us all a lesson not only in shrewdness but in Christianity.

It was a lesson that ended the revolution in the Philippines.

In the United States, where I had been returned by President Quirino at the beginning of 1952 with the portfolio of Ambassador to Washington added to my role as permanent delegate to the United Nations, I received disturbing reports of the growing tension between Quirino and Magsaysay. The political duckling that Quirino had nourished was developing into an eagle.

The reports grew more disturbing through the year and into 1953. Magsaysay increased in stature and success. The President commented more than once, "This man Magsaysay is getting too ambitious."

Magsaysay was ambitious. He knew there were many gaps in his political knowledge. But he was willing to learn. He had an open mind and would listen to many people and to all sides.

He made speeches in behalf of the Mindanao project and land reform, and they were simple, pungent speeches that drove straight to the hearts of the people.

He would say things like this: "I am proud to be a Filipino. We are a great people. With the right leadership and with the guidance and assistance of the United States this country can grow to be the head of a family of democratic nations in this part of the globe."

All that he was saying and doing was in behalf of the psychological warfare that was regaining the confidence of the people in their democracy. It was his contribution to the information sources being thrown open to the people by way of speeches, pamphlets, loyalty meetings, broadcasts, conferences, and rallies.

Everything was being done to win the great mass of the people completely away from the dangerous trend that had threatened for a time to wrest freedom from one of the few countries in Asia that was still free.

One of the strongest arguments for freedom was the success of the new settlements in Mindanao. That achievement won for Magsaysay a great deal of attention, both at home and abroad. He received honors and citations. The newspapermen liked him, and liked what he was doing. They wrote a great deal about him, and it was mostly praise. The newspapers of Manila were backing him in whatever he might do next.

He had the loyalty of the army, which had been revitalized as officers and men realized that their immediate chief was a man who could be trusted to protect them against evil, political, unmilitary influences, and who had driven favoritism out of the army so that promotions and activation were based again on merit and honor, and not on political pull. Officers could, and did, successfully defy impositions by political leaders, petty and national. The rank and file of the army were now convinced that their Secretary of Defense Magsaysay could be hard and inflexible, but that he infinitely preferred to be lenient, and he was always fair. To him, the Armed Forces was an instrument for the maintenance of the security of the nation, and he saw to it that it was given every care.

He had sent the army into action as a guardian of the people's most sacred right—the right of the free ballot, because he had seen that the forces of the government had to be committed against the forces of greed who were plotting to rob the people of their right to choose freely: he had so committed them.

The results of Magsaysay's brief tenure as Secretary of National Defense were far-reaching. First was the definite dissolution, temporary perhaps, but none the less decisive, of the Huks as a direct menace. Second, was the return of a sense of security among the people, and with it a regeneration of the people's belief that the government could be trusted and that democracy could survive. They had found in him an outstanding leader, who, having come from the masses, exercised his leadership by virtue of possessing the faith and confidence of the masses.

When the masses as in this case were Filipinos, traditionally steeped in the essence of individual liberty, which is the basic ideal of true democracy, then their combined, unwavering, spontaneously given faith is a force for a real man to count on—and for the enemies of freedom to fear.

Wherever he went crowds began gathering and cheering: "Mabuhay Magsaysay!" ("Long life, Magsaysay"); while the muttering against the government, which had not improved or changed its ways, grew more angry, and because anger must have a victim, it centered on the central figure of the government, which was President Quirino.

The "get-rich-quick boys" around the President chose a victim in their turn. Someone had to take the blame for the awakening of the people. They blamed Magsaysay.

So on the negative side the Magsaysay success in behalf of his Republic concentrated against him all of the forces of greed, of evil influence, of political intrigue, whose hitherto uninterrupted progress toward complete seizure of the national wealth Magsaysay's policies and decisive actions had so effectively stopped.

So it was that in 1953 Magsaysay and the people on one

hand, and, on the other, the administration and the forces behind it—forces of political influence against the best interests of the people—came into sharp and direct conflict. The Quirino regime which Magsaysay and his rejuvenated armies had saved from overthrow turned against him. For weeks, all he had accomplished was subjected to withering, relentless attack. Less and less frequently was he consulted as a member of the Cabinet. More and more frequently was he ignored and slighted.

The new settlements at Mindanao came under the ugliest barrage of criticism. They were called foolish and unnecessary by many top politicos, while Quirino had held all along that the Huks deserved bullets, not gifts of land. Everything Magsaysay had accomplished was belittled. Now that the danger of Communism was abated, the crooks close to power lifted their voices against the man who had done the most toward stopping that danger.

Meanwhile, as if in compensation, Magsaysay's popularity continued to grow with the common people and with all who had the real interests of the country at heart.

Quirino was disturbed by the soaring popularity of Magsaysay. The President was about to run for re-election. But now he was told that to the cry, "Long life to Magsaysay," people were beginning to add a new phrase, and were shouting, "Long life to our next president, Magsaysay!"

This was a situation no president about to run again could approve. The coldness grew between the two men. Magsaysay was pressing his land-reform measures which he felt were the answer to the claims of Communism.

159

Quirino belittled the reforms and snubbed Magsaysay deliberately on various occasions.

The break between the President and his Secretary of Defense was absolute.

That February Magsaysay resigned.

Chapter X

IN Washington, this April of 1953, I received an urgent call from Manila. President Quirino wanted me home at once for consultation.

I had an idea what he wanted of me, and I spent many a sleepless night before leaving. From Washington and the United Nations I had a wide view of what was happening to the free world. The Red danger was growing stronger every day. The threat of Communism was everywhere, even here in the United States. Next door, in Guatemala, the angry Red clouds were gathering rapidly, in the year 1953.

The Red wave had been halted in the Philippines. Was that a temporary setback to Russia? One knew the Communists would not give up that easily. And now that Magsaysay had resigned, we heard that graft was shooting up with renewed vigor around Malacañan. The forces of greed that had been stopped for a time were on the rampage again, determined to get all they could before the last of the booty was gone. The upsurge of corruption as always would be accompanied by the upsurge of Communism. That pair were bedfellows.

Some word of all these developments, so vital in import

to the survival of Western democracy in Asia, and, by implication, of such critical significance to the United States, was filtering through the news screen to the front pages in the United States. I use the word "screen" not to imply censorship, but to indicate that the voluminous reports from Korea, from Indochina, from Europe, as well as the mass of domestic material normal in a Presidential election year, practically monopolized the American newspapers. Because Magsaysay, with his clear, effective program against the active Communist threat, had attained the stature of a new and dramatic Asian figure, he had received a great deal of world-wide publicity. The American people had been made increasingly aware of what was happening to their wartime ally on the other side of the Pacific. But, purely as news, the reports of the graft-ridden regime in Manila could not be expected to compete with the high drama of Korea, or with the breath-taking developments in the Republican and Democratic parties here at home in America.

But to me, serving in Washington as the Philippine Ambassador, and in the United Nations as the permanent delegate of the Philippines, all that I read in public and private reports, and the concern I detected in the President's voice over the trans-Pacific radiophone as he ordered me home, were deeply disturbing.

My position at this time was not the most enviable. As Ambassador to the United States and as the United Nations delegate I was in theory representing my country. But in both instances, formally and as a matter of official record, I was a representative of my government—in short, of the existing administration of President Quirino.

Though removed by ten thousand miles from the actual scenes of the disturbances, I was both *de facto* and *de jure* a part of the regime that was causing the disturbances. Yet without a specific order from Manila there was nothing I could do save carry out my official duties with as brave a face as I could wear under the circumstances. I was hungry for action, and willing to do anything that would help put an end to the dangerous situation left by the withdrawal of Magsaysay.

Elementary tenets of ordinary loyalty had precluded any action on my part inimical to the administration until I was able to see for myself and determine for myself that there would be justification for my taking action. What that action might be, I had no way of knowing. Meanwhile, in the United States I had no choice. I had to uphold my country's position before the world, no matter what my private misgivings might be.

The call from Manila I knew would open the way to change. It would bring on a crisis in my personal life if I learned that all that was rumored was true.

And still, I dreaded that change. As far as my own private affairs were concerned, I had every reason to be happy in the United States, which had been my second home since my university years. My wife had made over the Embassy in Washington into a home of great comfort and beauty. She had brought from Manila paintings, furniture, and furnishings of every kind, all made in the Philippines, so that our Embassy was a bit of Filipino culture here in America. Our two younger sons were with us in Washington, attending school, while the two older boys were in Manila, launching careers of their own. We had many friends in the United States and our lives were again happy as in Manila before the war.

The refurbishing and refurnishing of the Embassy had just been completed when the call came, and also, I had just received, in addition to my other duties, the ambassadorships to Mexico and Cuba, and I was preparing to set up embassies in these countries and commute to my various posts by plane.

The diplomatic and United Nations posts and all the good fortune that had come to my family and to me since Bataan fell were sources of great happiness and satisfaction, and it was with a heavy heart that I suspended work in the United Nations in New York and in the Washington Embassy and halted the plans for the embassies in Havana and Mexico City.

With the greatest reluctance I interrupted the work in the United Nations. There I felt that I was not only fighting Communism, but I was voicing the aspirations of millions of voiceless Asians. Whenever an Asian problem came up I found myself debating against Vishinsky. It must have been an effective struggle, because when recently I had been nominated by the United States Government as Secretary-General of the United Nations, Vishinsky had announced that he was under specific orders from his own government to veto my name as often as it came up, and he served notice on the United States chief delegate not to submit my name any more as it would be useless. In a way, I had considered this a victory.

Other plans of vital importance to the Philippines were interrupted by the summons home at this particular time.

Let it not be forgotten that the problems besetting the Philippines in the United States were by no means minor. The gravest was the approach of the application of the terms of the Bell Act, when American tariffs on Philippine goods would begin to be imposed. The Quirino administration had done nothing—literally nothing—despite my insistent requests, toward preparing for the renegotiating of the Act, which is in effect the extant treaty of trade and commerce between the two nations. All the negotiations had been left in my hands, and my departure from Washington at this time would leave the whole issue hanging in the air.

Evidently what was rushing me home was far more serious, at least from President Quirino's point of view.

I knew that what he wanted of me had something to do with the coming election. He wanted to be re-elected President. But this year he was faced by an opponent who evidently had the love and trust of the people—his own former Secretary of Defense, Ramón Magsaysay.

When Magsaysay, a Liberal like Quirino, resigned as Secretary of Defense on February 28, he bolted the Liberal Party to run against Quirino on the Nationalist Party ticket. There had been two possible candidates in the latter party, Dr. José Laurel and Claro M. Recto, a brilliant dialectician. Laurel had opposed Quirino for the Presidency in the "dirty election." Both these candidates had withdrawn in favor of the popular Ramón Magsaysay, and on April 12 Magsaysay had been nominated Nationalist candidate for the Presidency.

This was real opposition for Quirino. This was why he

wanted me home. He had an idea I might be able to help him defeat Magsaysay.

Magsaysay had, of course, deserted our party in order to run for election. Like Quirino, and formerly Magsaysay, I belonged to the Liberals. Naturally, I wanted to fight on my party's side, if a fight would be necessary, and I feared it would be. But would I want to fight for my party if it harbored people unfavorable to the good of my country, and at the same time fight against the man who had been the biggest single force against Communism that we had ever had in the Philippines?

I left the United States with a heavy heart.

My oldest son Carlos, known as Mike, met me at the Manila Airport to drive me to our new home in the suburbs where the two oldest boys were living. Mike had just set up law practice in Manila.

Four months before, as a Christmas gift, I had sent him a Ford from the United States. I wanted to know why he had not come to meet me in the new car.

Mike scowled. "It's still in customs. I'd have to grease palms to get it out, and I made up my mind I wouldn't pay graft. So they still have the car."

I knew then that the worst I had heard was true. If they would dare do this to my son, a practicing attorney whose father was in the government, what were they doing to those who had no voice at all, no means with which to protest?

That was only the first glimpse. Wherever I went I heard sneering, ugly words against the government. Little boys playing in the streets warned one another against cheating saying, "Don't Quirino me."

This, from the mouths of children, against the head of the State!

The sense of hatred was everywhere. I came in for my share as a member of the government. This was a different country. These were a divided people. I was a stranger in a country that was strange to me.

Physically, Manila had improved since my last visit home. The city, eighty per cent of which had been ruined by the Japanese, was rebuilding; the American war damage claims had helped in that. The Spanish walled city was still in rubble and the beautiful ancient churches were gone, but the other sections had been improved in the rebuilding. The new buildings were modern and handsome structures, and the streets had been widened. Out of ruin had come new advantages and greater beauty for the capital of the Philippines.

But tension was in the streets. It hung like fog over Manila, the "Pearl of the Orient."

I learned that the President was always surrounded by bodyguards; tanks guarded the Palace.

I spoke to an old man in charge of a toll gate. He was respectable and dignified, as are our old men of the Philippines. Out of curiosity I asked him, "What do you think of President Quirino?"

He spat into the dust at his feet. "That———"

He spoke in Ilocano. It was an insulting word in the President's own dialect! That a Filipino should speak in such a way of the head of the State was as incomprehensible to me as it was shocking. Filipinos are not like that! Courtesy and respect are absorbed with their mother's milk. Only when they have lost all respect for that which they have revered, or when Communism takes possession of their minds, do they change.

The whole horrible picture became clear in a very few days. The approaching election was racing the Filipinos toward civil war. If the evil regime continued and without the restraining hand of Magsaysay, Communism would be revived and would take over.

The angry mutterings were audible to anyone willing to listen. The anger centered upon one word: Change!

The cry for change was everywhere. But it was not heard in the muted halls of Malacañan or on the comfortable Presidential yacht, the *Apo*, idling on the waters of Manila Bay.

On the first day of May, President Quirino and I had a long talk aboard the *Apo* where he had invited me for dinner. The President was worried, and he was frank in stating his worries. He had called me back from the United States, he said, because he wanted to run again for President of the Philippines and to win, and he knew he had a formidable opponent in Magsaysay.

I told the President as frankly, since he wanted my opinion, that I thought his decision to run a second time was inadvisable in view of the temper of the people. They wanted change. They wanted a new leader.

They were asking for Magsaysay.

The President pointed out that Magsaysay was no longer a Liberal and was therefore against our party. He wanted the Liberal Party to remain in power. To help it stay there he had recalled me to the Philippines. He thought I could help him if I ran with him on the Liberal Party ticket as candidate for Senator.

168

The President pointed out that I had many friends. Many Filipinos trusted in my word. He was certain that with my help he could defeat Magsaysay.

I wondered if the President had forgotten that he was able to be aboard this yacht again without fear of being captured by the Huks only because of Magsaysay. The President's life, like the lives of all the Filipino people, had been made safer and more free by the man who had just bolted from the Liberal Party to run against him in the coming election of 1953.

We all owed much to Magsaysay.

I told the President what I honestly thought—that he should not seek the nomination. I told him to follow the example of ex-President Truman. I emphasized to him that I felt for the good of the country he should not seek re-election.

My mind may have been made up even then. I had been home only a few days, but already I had been forced to the conclusion that the leadership of the Liberal Party, which had been in control of the government since 1946 when independence began, had so deteriorated, so degenerated into a virtual dictatorship of vested, graft-ridden, corruption-impelled interests, that a complete change of leadership was essential if we were to secure a democratic government capable of safeguarding the rights, the liberties, and the heritage of the Filipino people.

The President switched to another method of approach. He told me he wanted to continue the fight against Communism and to round out his economic development program, and he wanted me to help him with both jobs. He

169

became emotional as he pleaded with me not to let him down. He was, he said, a sick man.

I answered him point for point. I argued that we who had worked with him all these years were prepared by experience and background to carry out all projected plans. I told him the people demanded change and that it was dangerous not to listen. I repeated: "Mr. President, in your own as well as in the nation's interest, you must not insist upon another nomination."

He stood up. "You want to be President!" he charged me.

I reminded him that I had come to Manila at his insistent request, that I was content in Washington, and that to enter politics was farthest from my thoughts.

But his attitude changed. He said slowly and calmly: "I will withdraw in your favor if you run."

On that astonishing note the interview ended.

The following day he sent for me at Malacañan.

Nothing in his attitude hinted at our talk of the night before on the yacht. On the contrary, he made it appear that we were meeting for the first time since my return from Washington.

"I want you to head our Senatorial ticket," he said urgently. "You can lead our campaign to victory."

He seemed to think the matter was settled.

I refused to commit myself. By this time I was extremely puzzled.

During the next few days our home in the suburbs was the scene of many political conferences and of many silent wrestlings with my own conscience. This house in the Manila suburb of Makati, where I was staying with my two oldest sons, was a new home we had built since the liberation, for not a stick of furniture nor a plank had remained of our old home after the Japanese bombers did their work. The new house we named "Kasiyahan," which is the Tagalog word for "contentment." But there was little contentment in it for me these days.

The President, who had gone to vacation at Baguio, must have read in the papers that a Romulo-for-President movement was mushrooming in the provinces, and he sent for me again.

I asked Congressman José J. Roy to drive to Baguio with me. But when we reached the mountain resort, Quirino had departed for his seaside hide-away at Poro Point, and left word we were to follow him there.

At the Point I was amazed when Quirino opened the conversation by recalling our conference on board the *Apo,* which I thought he had completely forgotten. He told Congressman Roy he was willing to withdraw in my favor if I chose to run. "But I want to be nominated first," he told us. "You can see I am not a well man. After my nomination I may have to go to the United States for medical attention. Then, I will designate Romulo as the candidate."

This sounded like a simple plan. But Roy, a veteran politician, was cautious. "In that case, Mr. President, General Romulo would not be the convention's candidate but your personal candidate," he argued. And to me he whispered, "It won't work."

Quirino then took up his previous refrain. It was imperative that I head the senatorial ticket of the Liberal Party. Once I was elected, he would see to it that I was made president of the Senate. And he asked me, "What is your decision?"

I told him that I would abide by the decision of the convention.

I added that once a decision was made on my part, I would not go behind his back; I would announce it to him face to face. In fact, he would be the first to know.

After we left the President, reporters asked him the results of our discussion. Quirino is fond of wisecracking. He said, "I told Romulo he could run for any position, from town councilor to President."

The reporters took him seriously. The result was stories published in all Manila papers headed: QUIRINO GIVES ROMULO THE GREEN SIGNAL which were displayed on front pages in Manila in banner headlines.

More telegrams, urging me to run for the Presidency, poured in from all over the country.

Quirino left his vacation hide-away and flew back to Manila. He told reporters who met him at the airport: "I will ship that s.o.b. back to Washington and make him pack up." When the reporters asked, "Who will take Romulo's place?" he answered, "Anyone can take his place."

The time for decision had come. I had promised Quirino not to go behind his back. Now I asked for an appointment to see him on the following afternoon, May 14.

That night, alone in my room in the house at Makati, on the portable typewriter that goes with me everywhere, I typed out my resignation.

I had not arrived at this momentous decision alone. With no effort on my part, a way had opened for me.

A few days after my return to Manila, while I was still dazed by Quirino's attitude, the change I found in the people, and their violent demand for a more constructive change, a small newspaper in an obscure island had come out with a headline ROMULO FOR PRESIDENT. The accompanying article stated that a club had been formed under that name.

The following day I began to receive hundreds of telegrams begging me to remain in the Philippines and run for the Presidency. Romulo-for-President clubs sprang up all over the provinces. Quirino's jesting comment gave them impetus.

The movement snowballed before I fully realized what was happening. A group of Senators and Congressmen announced their intention to back me, and headquarters were set up in the Manila Hotel. Still I was undecided and I could not tell my would-be sponsors whether or not I would accept the honor of candidacy. Even the matter of my resignation from my government posts remained in the air until the night before.

The night before I wrote out my resignation I had radio-telephoned Virginia in Washington. Her reaction was instantaneous. "If you are going to resign and retire and have a little rest—fine! But if you are going to resign and enter politics, please don't!"

I told her I had made up my mind. Her voice was gentle and understanding from ten thousand miles away. "Very well, then, if you have decided what you want to do, whatever it is will be all right with me."

I hung up thinking of her and the two youngsters asleep in the Embassy over there; we seemed very far apart.

173

What I faced might put an end to much of the happiness and comfort in our lives, and put an end also to the power for good that had been given to me.

That night I had a long talk with the two older boys. My sons are all frank to a painful degree in letting me know what is in their minds. When I hinted that I might resign, and worse still, run for the Presidency, they both declared emphatically that I was crazy.

I remembered again the beautiful Embassy in Washington, the United Nations buildings in New York, the new ambassadorships in Havana and Mexico City, and the even more influential life of a Senator, and I privately agreed with the boys—I would be crazy to throw all this away for a precarious future.

Gregorio, who is a university professor of economics and is conservative, pointed out that I would be wasting all the years of struggle in exchange for an illusion. Mike was even more realistic. Both lads had fought as boy-guerrillas through the Japanese occupation; they had gone to school in Manila; they had stayed in touch with the mood of their generation and their country. Mike, attacking the problem as an attorney, pointed out certain obstacles in my way in crisp logic.

"In the first place, you're completely out of touch with the Philippines," he said. "You've spent the years since the war in the United States and you have no idea what the people over here are thinking."

I argued that democratic people thought the same way the world over and that I had found people in the Philippines and in America much the same.

But Mike wasn't listening. "You haven't a chance to be

President. You have no party behind you and you have no money. Why, it would take five million pesos at least to put over a fight like that, and where are you going to raise that much money!"

Then the boys softened a little. They pointed out the difficult postwar years and the struggle to redeem the losses suffered in war, the lecture tours and the writing, the long struggle on behalf of the Philippines in the legislative halls of Washington and around the conference tables of the United Nations. And they wound up by saying:

"You have world prestige, Dad, and you've won it the hard way. Why risk it all in a dirty political fight?"

At that time I really had no idea how dirty a political campaign can be, and how unfeeling and even brutal people can become when blinded by partisanship. But I told my boys that no matter what the consequences, my mind was made up. Even defeat would have its compensation in the thrill that goes with fighting for a cause in which one passionately believes.

"I realize the odds are stacked against me," I said, "but remember this: I have come back to Manila at a time that is crucial for our people. Here is a chance for me to serve at home. I don't want it said after I have passed away that you are the sons of a man who shirked his responsibility as a Filipino and who, instead of staying with his people at a time when he was most needed, preferred to go back to Washington, to live comfortably, write books, and make money. I will fight with all that is in me. If the people choose otherwise, no one can ever say that I turned my back on them."

They saw it was useless to argue with me, and the following afternoon they went with me to Malacañan.

It was 5:15 when we left the campaign headquarters at the Manila Hotel, and drove to the Palace. I was grateful to have my sons with me on this day, which was one of the most crucial of my life.

The May sun sparkled over Manila and over Corregidor in the bay. On another day in another May, eleven years before, Corregidor had fallen. I was in Australia with General MacArthur on that tragic day.

This day seemed as sad to me. It was as if the personal sacrifice I was about to make was part of the long defeat and betrayal that we Filipinos had been made to suffer since achieving freedom.

The ugly metal shapes of tanks were deployed around Malacañan.

Inside the Palace I said good-bye to my sons and left them in the corridor outside the President's room with the request that they wait for me; I would not be long. Then I went in to meet the President, alone.

In everything I did I was trying to give an example of political maturity worthy of our new Republic. Nothing I was doing at this time was easy. It had not been an easy matter to decide to make this sacrifice. It was not easy to meet my President, face to face as I met him now, and give him the letter I took from my pocket and handed him in silence—a letter, let me say, that had literally been written in prayer and tears.

It is not easy to meet with the President of one's country and break with him.

I might have sent that letter to him by messenger or

by mail. It would have been easier for us both. But such an act would not have been politically mature. Too many attacks and counterattacks had marred our brief period of self-government. I had made my decision, and I was going to show my fellow Filipinos that a public official who breaks with his leader can do it in an honorable and dignified way.

President Quirino had an appointment to make a speech, but he read my letter of resignation through. Then he said, "Rommy, this is the most severe indictment against my administration . . ." He stopped in the middle of the sentence, picked up a napkin from a tray left on a table, and wiped his face with it. He seemed distraught. He dropped the letter onto the desk and went to his bedroom. A little later he came back, took up the letter again and put it into his pocket. He had nothing more to say.

I thanked him for all the personal considerations he had shown me and told him I would always be grateful, and I offered my hand. At first he hesitated then took it reluctantly, saying, "I accept your resignation. Immediately."

I told him, "Mr. President, my first attack against you will be made over the radio tonight at nine o'clock."

Then I hurried out to tell the boys and to telephone Virginia.

My letter of resignation to His Excellency Elpidio Quirino, President of the Philippines, written on May 14, 1953, reads, in part, as follows:

Dear Mr. President:

On board the *Apo* on May 1, the evening following my return to Manila at your behest, you spoke to me frankly about the reasons why you have decided to seek the nomination of our party for the second term. I informed you then that in my considered opinion it would be desirable in the national interest that you reconsider your decision to seek another term.

This statement . . . rests upon the sober, impersonal conviction which I have reached that a change in leadership would not only be a good thing for the country at this time, but is indeed an essential condition for our future progress.

. It also rests upon the equally sober realization that our people profoundly desire such a change.

Our people today are weary and confused. If they are not demoralized, it is because of the inherent spiritual power and the unshakable faith which has distinguished them throughout the ages, through which they have always been able to recruit renewed strength of purpose to overcome the mightiest obstacles to their progress.

Despite the restoration of a degree of economic stability, economic difficulties among our masses have been mounting. Economic inequalities have become more noticeable. These, with their natural concomitants—political confusion, social decay and above all, a noticeably growing lack of public confidence in government—have created a situation of grave national peril that is unprecedented in our history, and that has brought deep concern to all thinking men who have been witnesses of these phenomena.

It has not been easy for me, Mr. President, to reach the conclusion that has been forced on me by factors and stresses visible to so many of our countrymen, that our people are in a deep discontent under a burden of woes and grievances.

178

These considerations have compelled me to the conclusion that the time has come for a salutary and necessary change in the leadership of our national life—one which will remove from the palate of our people the stale taste of promises unfulfilled, or failures, and will provide the people with fresh resolve and inspiration, based on a reinvigorated faith in government.

And here lies the crux of the present specific political situation, the implication of which candor compels me to note for your consideration. It cannot have escaped you that bitter feelings have been engendered: and it is my conviction, shared by many, that a supreme gesture by you—a gesture not so much of self-abnegation as of a vision that rises above the level of the moderately enlightened—would act to dissolve these feelings in a solvent of national good will and understanding, and would avert consequences which you would be the first to deplore.

Such an act on your part, all circumstances considered, would shine as an act of enlightened statesmanship and patriotism, would constitute a heartening recognition of our democracy's inherent capacity for renewal, and would establish you in a position of high moral leadership and influence which no mere political effort could give.

I have addressed this letter to you in complete candor, out of a sense of patriotic duty. To tell you the unvarnished truth is, I believe, the highest form of service that I can render the party now. What happens to me personally is a matter of little consequence. It is the future of our country that is paramount. On this, I am certain, we agree.

I am cognizant of the fact that by suggesting, as I do now, that you forbear, in the national interest, from seeking nomination or election for another term, I am creating a situation in which you may feel that I no longer am capable of that complete meeting of minds which would make my continuance as your Ambassador to the United

States, and Permanent Delegate to the United Nations, possible.

For this reason I hereby have the honor to place in your hands my resignation from both posts.

Sincerely yours,

CARLOS P. ROMULO

When I left the President's room after tendering my resignation I found my sons waiting in the corridor. They took one look at my face, then Mike was pumping my hand and Greg was pounding my shoulder.

"We didn't think you'd do it! We're proud of you, Dad!"

We walked out of the Palace shoulder to shoulder— three free men.

The world seemed to have slipped off my back; a burden of years. For the first time in years I had the feeling that now I could do something to serve the very soul of my country. No matter what happened to me, what I did would be done for the people of the Philippines.

The first thing to do was get to a telephone and call Virginia in Washington. It was past six in the evening in Manila, which is past six in the morning in Washington. The two youngest boys, Dick and Bobby, were still sleeping but Virginia was awake and waiting for my call. I told her: "Pack everything and get out. Do not let anyone order you out of the Embassy!"

Evidently Bobby had been wakened, and I heard him running into her room and clamoring to speak. I heard her say, "Bobby, your father has resigned," then to me, "Bobby wants to speak to you." I could picture him, tousle-headed and in his pajamas, and imagine the grin on his face as he took up the phone.

180

Bobby yelled, "Congratulations, Mister Private Citizen!"

Due to the extravagant kindnesses paid me both in America and the Philippines, I had just been awarded my twenty-seventh university degree, and the numerous ribbons and medals while sacred to me are often the subject of hilarity with my boys, so many there are, but I consider Bobby's words my finest citation.

After hanging up I went directly to the headquarters in the Manila Hotel. The place was filled with men who were my proffered sponsors all eager to know what had taken place in the Palace. I told them, "The die is cast." There was exultation, and they crowded around me, Senators and Congressmen among them, exclaiming, "Our Candidate! Now we have a candidate!"

I was giving up much that I had worked hard for and valued for the right to enter the turgid and turbulent political sea.

I was the perfect novice. I had never been in politics. I had been a newspaperman when circumstances had catapulted me into the army; another change, and I had landed in the diplomatic world. But I had never known political life at close range. My activities when I campaigned in behalf of the Bell Act—when the bomb had been thrown—had until this time been my only contact with politics.

It seemed perfectly simple to me. I believed that all I had to do was to give people the truth; they would understand.

As for the men who were around me in that moment, pledging their loyalty, I would remember later that it

181

seems a universal law in politics that he who most loudly protests his loyalty will be the first to turn.

I may have had some inkling then, for once the handshaking was over I told them, "I don't know how many of you will stick by me, but I am in this fight to the bitter end."

Virginia was wasting no time in Washington after our trans-Pacific conversation ended. She and the two boys were packed and out of the Embassy within twenty-four hours.

At nine o'clock that evening I read my letter of resignation to President Quirino on a national broadcast. I may say that an entire nation was shocked. Now there was no backing out.

One week later Virginia and the two younger boys arrived in Manila. By that time, I was off campaigning on the island of Mindanao.

Meanwhile Ramón Magsaysay was well launched on his own campaign.

I did not know Magsaysay very well, but I had the highest regard for his sincerity, his energy, and his integrity. I realized what a daring thing he had done in taking a stand against Quirino. He was risking everything, even his life. So deeply hated was he by the racketeers that it was rumored they would go to any length to stop him, and also, there were the crooks in power who would let nothing stand in their way. He had no money with which to carry on his campaign, and now that he had resigned as Secretary of Defense he had no income at all, no power in his hands.

182

If he lost, he would lose everything.

Apparently he was facing the future with cheerfulness and good humor. He and his pretty wife Luz and the three small children had moved into a small house in the suburbs, together with a small zoo of family pets, which included eight tiny deer. There was no furniture at first, but Magsaysay had the love of many people, and many came to him bringing gifts of pieces of furniture, rice, vegetables, fruits, and fowl. In return, the Magsaysays welcomed all who came and fed them. Hospitality is a Filipino tradition. One heard of the Magsaysay household as running over with good cheer.

From this haven he conducted his campaign, which was to, and for, the people. The big smiling man in the Filipino shirt and slacks was driving around the country, walking through rice paddies and terraced vegetable gardens, holding long, neighborly conversations in the dialects that were the speech of his childhood.

Two arguments kept me from offering my services to Magsaysay. As I say, I did not know him, but I knew that he was not well read, he had little knowledge of any country outside his own—he could not, it was said, name many of the heads of other countries. His relative inexperience in the larger aspects of the government and in world affairs at a time when the exigencies of the international situation faced a country so strategically placed as the Philippines made me doubt Magsaysay, not for his ability, but for his lack of experience.

He had the faith of the people. Was this enough?

He had proved himself a great policeman and a splendid soldier. But as political head? As President?

There were many who felt he was not seasoned enough, not experienced enough, to lead the Republic. Not knowing Magsaysay, but knowing of his limitations, I agreed with them, and said so publicly.

This appraisal, together with a natural and understandable feeling of loyalty to the party with which I had been affiliated since the days of the late President Roxas, decided me against supporting Magsaysay and led me instead to seek the nomination of the Liberal Party, Quirino's own party.

There were others willing and eager to run against Quirino. We knew that he had evidence against them all which he was planning to use if they offered their names. One had accepted a bribe, another was mixed up in a building deal, and so on. Against me, he had nothing.

I determined to challenge him. I knew what it would mean to me if I lost. It was no easy decision to make.

But even if I lost, the very fact that someone had dared challenge him would weaken his power.

The important need was to change the leadership. To change the leadership meant to dethrone Quirino. He controlled the powerful Liberal Party. The only chance of breaking that control was to run against him.

Also, not being of the stuff of angels, my own personal ambitions were involved. Beyond all else I longed to be President of the Philippines. President Osmeña had wanted me to run as his Vice President; I had declined. I could have run as Vice President with Roxas, when he also had asked me; and then, when Roxas died——but all that was water under the bridge. Quirino had run in my place, and it was he who had become President by virtue of disaster. He had piled disaster upon disaster, not because he was evil, for Quirino has no evil in him, but because he had not been strong enough to deny the rights of corruption to those who were close to him.

I firmly believed that owing to my years of experience in the United States, which had given us its concept of our democracy, and the years of experience in the United Nations, I would be able to give the Philippines an intelligent and honest government. I had served under four presidents and felt that I had been through the mill. Patriotism had its part in my decision; I was being forced into it by circumstances, not by politics.

I had returned to the Philippines at Quirino's request because it was my duty. A sense of duty had compelled me to leave him, and now, to challenge him.

With only ten days left before the national convention of the Liberal Party would select its candidate, I announced that I would seek the nomination against Quirino.

Now I had to get support, to try to swing the party behind me and win delegates to my side. I was the underdog and all the odds were against me.

There was much to be done in the next few days.

Chapter XI

IT was a strange campaign.

I was joined by Fernando Lopez, the Vice President under Quirino, a distinguished public servant who was one of the few in the higher echelons of the Liberal regime to divorce himself completely from the machinations and the intrigues of the high-party brass. By joining me he abandoned and publicly condemned the tempting promises of high-party patronage.

One by one, I challenged the delegates. They were fearful. Intelligence was reporting all my movements to Quirino. I visited them by night in their homes, and it always seemed to be raining on those nights. A few refused to see me; they were afraid. But of eight hundred and eighty-six delegates to the convention, six hundred and forty-four gave me their pledges. I had the overwhelming majority!

By day I was making speeches. Senator Cabili went about with me day and night. The Senator, a seasoned campaigner, was amused, I think, by my fervor and inexperience. I was stumping the city and its environs in my own behalf wherever the delegates were, without thought for proper meals or sleep.

At the same time I was making every effort to insure a fair deal for myself at the convention of May 24. I knew that certain of Quirino's supporters, among whom were several relatives, would apply steam-roller tactics. I called these men his "Storm Troopers," and coined a slogan: "Quirino has foisted upon the people a Government of relatives, by relatives, and for relatives."

In the Philippines, a Presidential convention nominates either by secret ballot or *viva-voce* vote. Obviously, the latter would assure Quirino's nomination. The delegates would hardly dare defy him openly, since they were carefully chosen by Liberal leaders, and many of them held appointive posts subject to Presidential pleasure. That was why I had polled the delegates in secret, and why Senator Cabili was seeking approval of rules in the convention which would call for a secret vote.

That also was why I had dared risk competing against Quirino with so short a time in which to prepare. If a secret vote were taken I would win, and the secret vote is a democratic procedure. If Quirino refused to accept a secret-ballot rule, he would sustain his first moral defeat in the eyes of the people. That would be the first step toward a change of leadership which I now regarded as essential. It would in itself make my efforts worth while.

All this was undertaken in ten days.

When I entered the convention hall for the Liberal Party convention, I was given a standing ovation that brought tears to my eyes. I shook hands with each delegate. The majority were for me. They had pledged their word.

Quirino was not there. He was a sick man, under med-

187

ical care in the Palace. The thought crossed my mind then that Quirino had already been President for six years and that if he had the good of the country at heart he would have deferred. I think he might have deferred if only those close to him who were getting richer all the time had not persuaded him to run again.

The hall was jammed with delegates. The Quirino group had used army planes to bring delegates from all the provinces. Two hotels in Manila had been set aside in which to entertain them.

What chance had I against such organized power!

I looked them over and recognized those who had hired the gunmen to keep the people from the polls in the "dirty election" of 1949, and who had grown rich at the expense of the Republic. They were making no attempt to hide their feelings toward me.

What followed was picturesquely described in blow-by-blow accounts over the radio and in the press. Senator Tomás Cabili skillfully and forcefully argued on the floor for an open vote. He was ably seconded by Congressman José J. Roy of Tarlac. But a proposal for a voice vote was steamrollered, with every kind of palpable intimidation of delegates, by the opposition, led by two of Quirino's brothers—one the governor of a province, the other a tycoon. Under this bludgeoning, a docile gathering submitted.

At two o'clock in the afternoon—direct from the Palace —the unprecedented order was given for an open vote!

I knew then—when the open vote was ordered and the two brothers of Quirino were among the canvassers—that my chances were gone.

I stared about me, from face to face—at men I had been certain were for me—who had given me their promises of support, and even been the first to urge me to run against Quirino.

Their faces were turned away. The shock of dismay and despair was deep, but through it came a sense of gloating. This proved that Quirino was afraid! The delegates were not to blame. They dared not vote for anyone but Quirino under the pitiless publicity of the open vote that he and his henchmen had ordered.

This moment of both triumph and despair was the time to strike. Senator Cabili claimed the floor as soon as the vote was taken, with the majority, of course, pro-Quirino. I stood up and left the convention hall. "This is the greatest injustice," Senator Cabili began. "If you cannot give justice to men of your own party, how can you give justice to the people?"

He prophesied then that although President Quirino had won the nomination he would lose the election. Then he, Congressman Roy, Senator Lorenzo Sumulong, highly regarded for his ability and integrity, and others walked out of the convention hall, and a powerful section of the Liberal Party went with us, including Vice President Fernando Lopez, who as a result was subsequently to lose his own bid for renomination on the Liberal ticket.

Later events were to uphold Senator Cabili's forecast that this challenge to the Quirino regime on the secret-ballot rule and my bolting the convention and the party were moral blows to the Quirino program that would eventually contribute to his ignominious defeat and the almost complete collapse of the Liberal Party. These two incidents were eye-openers to the people. They showed that no regime was sacrosanct; that a man could be challenged, no matter how high or entrenched his position.

Now we were left on the outside, with no party or organization of our own. But it was not too late to make one last fight for the change which, after all, was my main objective. The logical result of the events of that convention day was the founding, that very night, of a new party of our own, the Democratic Party, with its sole purpose the defeat of the Quirino regime. One week later I drew up its platform, and on its ticket I continued the campaign for the Presidency of the Philippines. My original reasons for seeking the nomination still held good, although now I would of necessity have to count on votes drafted from both parties.

We all worked hard, with a sense of righteousness to sustain us. And as the new party's campaign manager, we chose Congressman Raul Leuterio, for twelve years Floor Leader of the majority party in the House, a master political tactician.

This was my first campaign. For two months I campaigned in Luzon, the Visayas, Mindanao. I did what Magsaysay was doing, I went to the barrios, to the Filipino people. It was out in these places in the Philippines that I saw a Philippines I had never known before, and it was here that I saw the dangerous workings of Communism in its beginnings at the edges of a country, driving its way toward its heart. I realized what inroads into the thought of the people had been made by the Huks, who as we knew so well by this time were the organized Communists. The seeds of poison had been well planted. The first crop had been shorn, but the roots remained.

Bitterness toward the Quirino regime, toward the government, which to the people was democracy—this kept alive the deep and secret roots. People were still remembering, in their hearts, that the Huks had promised justice where the government gave none. They had asked for change. What next, if there were no change?

This I learned in the barrios, and also I learned that I was splitting the Presidential vote. The people who came to my meetings were the people who had attended the meetings of Magsaysay, and afterward many would come to me and say that while before they had been for Magsaysay, now they would vote for me. They told me of Magsaysay clubs being disbanded and Romulo clubs being formed.

It became increasingly clear that far from destroying Quirino I was strengthening him by weakening his opponent. This was reviving hope in the remaining Huks.

My purpose had been to change leadership and fight Communism. I found I was not doing that by insisting upon my candidacy.

It was time to stop and think things over.

This was a poor man's campaign I was conducting. I had spent all my reserves, built up by writing and lecturing in the years since Bataan. My wife had reason to be indignant: "See, you worked and slaved and it is all going!" I told her, "I'm not afraid of financial ruin. What I am afraid of is the perpetuation of an administration that will ruin our country."

As always, she saw things my way.

During the last two weeks of the campaign I was practically penniless. I was driving from barrio to barrio, often with barely enough money to get me to the next town. This I told to the country people, and they began bringing money, two centavos, perhaps, or five. In the province of Quezon, formerly Tayabas (renamed because Quezon was born there), I was speaking in one small town and found myself without means to buy gasoline to go on to the next, where I was scheduled to speak. I told the audience, and they dug down into their pockets and came up with thirty-two pesos, enough to send me on to the neighboring province.

But it was not lack of funds that first made me consider withdrawing from the race. I might have carried on. There were certain willing supporters to be counted on who did not want me to stop.

Again I had to make a decision that was not an easy one. It was based upon cold calculation. It took into consideration only the final results to the Filipino people.

It was plain by this time that both Magsaysay and I would be defeated and as a fatal result the Quirino forces would remain in power. Corruption would return full blast, the same conditions would generate again, and the Huks, with Magsaysay powerless to stop them, would rise again. Another four years of graft and corruption could result only in revolution, which in this case would be Communism.

Magsaysay had shown that he knew how Communists can be fought. He had recognized the fact that to kill Communism the navel string had to be cut between the Huks and the people. The splendid job he had done as

Secretary of Defense had put the Huks under control. Many had been killed, thousands had been forced to surrender, others had voluntarily given up their arms. But the basic conditions Magsaysay had not been able to correct, because he lacked the power.

He had been able to establish the semblance of law and order, but the roots of disturbance were still there, and what were these roots but the misery and oppression felt by the people, while the Huks, quiescent, were waiting, still in hiding, in scattered groups. Luis Taruc, their leader, was still at large.

Now, if Magsaysay remained cut off from all authority, it would not take long for the Huks to assume control.

The powers in office had blocked Magsaysay's every effort. He had been obliged to resign as Secretary of Defense to run for the principles he thought were right.

If Quirino won, Magsaysay would be permanently out of the way. He would be a man without a job and without power. The Philippines would be left undefended, without order or law. And Quirino was winning. My campaign was helping him win.

To supplant the Quirino administration, one of us, either Magsaysay or myself, would have to win. To win, one of us, either he or I, would have to give way.

Midway in my own campaign, I pondered all that Magsaysay had done and all he was doing, and tried to evaluate impersonally the man who was fighting the shoestring campaign to become President of the Philippines.

Without money or power behind him, Magsaysay had gone directly to the people. He was one of the people. He was native—and when had we had a great native leader in our part of Asia? Our other Filipino leaders, as one looked back, had a preponderance of foreign blood, which is to say, none had been pure Malayan. The Spanish forebears of Quezon, and of Roxas, had left their dominant characteristics on both these men. The Chinese blood of Osmeña marked his dignified, scholarly mien. Quirino was part Spanish and part Chinese. All had been accustomed to money and luxury. But Magsaysay was Malayan. He was of the land and of the people. He went about among them hatless, wearing his shirt outside his trousers as the Filipino wears his shirt, for coolness and comfort, sharing his problems and theirs, making jokes. He knew how to take a joke on himself and turn it into an asset.

When Quirino's supporters had circulated photostatic copies of Magsaysay's record in the University of the Philippines, showing that Magsaysay had flunked practically all his subjects and been obliged to leave school, the people were delighted. "See!" they chuckled. "He is not perfect. He is one of us."

He had no fluency of speech. He was not an orator. The people did not mind. Many a Filipino said to me with delight, "See, Magsaysay cannot speak easily; he is like me, he cannot express what he feels."

In his speeches, this diamond in the rough would tell with amusement of his first ventures into government halls, and how the rugs in Malacañan were so beautiful that on his first visits he had not believed they were to be stepped on, so he walked carefully around them. His office, when he was in an office, had always been open to all who came, and sometimes when talking he slipped off his shoes and put his feet up on his desk, because he could talk better that way.

And the people laughed at such things, and because he did them, they loved Magsaysay.

All he had was the love of the people. I had wondered, was that enough?

Evidently Magsaysay thought it was. He had staked his future, his family's security, and even his own life, on the faith of the people. He had given up his powerful position for the chance to help these troubled people who had been the first to cheer him in the streets in their mutual Ilocano or Tagalog as their future President. That cry had come from the pavements and the dusty roads, from rice paddies, from the doorways of nipa huts and small shops all over the Philippines. It was not a weak cry. It had force in it, and the threat of violence if left unheeded.

Leaders are never created. In an emergency, in the moment critical, they appear for good or evil, as leaders of the people. It is that irrefutable logic of the masses, which to the sophisticated may seem senseless and stupid, but which in the end is nearly always shown to be right, that which creates the media in which these men appear. The intuition of the people runs on direct lines toward human betterment. That was proven in France when men fought with sticks at the Bastille against the trained soldiers of King Louis, and in America's thirteen Colonies when the teabags were emptied into Boston Harbor. How the effete British sneered at Washington's ragged masses! How the French aristocrats fanned their noses as they drove through the silent watchful mobs in Paris! And in the Philippines we, too, had given proof of the righteous

195

intuition of the masses when, in a critical moment in our history, the uncultured plebeian Andres Bonifacio had urged the people into tearing up on a historic midnight the cedulas—the poll-tax receipts—an act of defiance against Spain that launched our Revolution. That simple gesture on the part of the unarmed and oppressed Filipino people had been the first move for freedom against Spain —Spain, that had then the most powerful army in the world!

Here in another critical moment another such man was needed and there were many who thought they saw him in Magsaysay.

Senator Laurel, the unquestioned Nationalist Party leader, when he had nominated Ramón Magsaysay as the candidate for the Presidency at the national convention, compared him to our revolutionary leader Bonifacio. Laurel, whose selflessness and humility have won my respect and admiration, said that day of Magsaysay:

"I wasn't looking for a wise man or a sage. I was looking for an honest man with guts."

Laurel and Recto, the two leaders of the Nationalists, were to have been the party candidates. They had deferred in favor of Magsaysay.

I was to defer likewise, two months later, in the very midst of my campaign.

It was the most difficult decision I have ever made. Withdrawal was in a way defeat. It put me back where I had started, with nothing left. As I say, I might have campaigned on, but I thought it fairer to change leadership by helping Magsaysay.

It meant a real sacrifice, material as well as moral, for

me to withdraw from the race. I had to think not only of myself and my family but of the many notable men who had risked everything to throw in their lot with mine. The Philippine political system of parties, of party loyalties and of party rewards, is closely patterned on the American system. I would not be the only one left on the outside, without a future or a source of income.

But as against my personal inclinations, which were to continue the fight to the end no matter how bitter, was the main consideration: that the leadership of my country had to be changed if freedom were to survive.

For that reason I deferred in favor of Magsaysay.

When I returned to my home after making the announcement of withdrawal it was like entering a place of mourning. The rooms were filled with weeping people. Many spoke to me with reproach and tears. "General, why did you abandon us? We risked everything to help you. It is not fair."

I felt worse than anyone there.

The next day my car was stopped in the middle of Taft Avenue by a crowd of students. Their young faces were hurt, reproachful. "General, why did you do this to us? Why did you let us down?"

I had to find a way to explain. As always, my only medium was the platform. I wanted to tell everyone why I had given way to Magsaysay, and why I felt he was the man to meet this crisis between Communism and democratic freedom. To me, personally, my first opinion that Ramón Magsaysay lacked something of the experience in the international field which the times demanded, had been overbalanced by his intense integrity, his command-

197

ing personality, his deep sense of obligation to the cause of the people, and his sense of humility, which enabled him to seek and to accept honestly proffered advice. These more than compensated for his lack of political experience.

A proposal was made and accepted to unite the two opposition parties, the Nationalist and the Democratic, in a coalition which would preserve the identity of both parties while uniting their resources in the campaign for clean government.

Then I found another decision had to be made. I was offered the post of national campaign manager for the coalition! Magsaysay was waiting for an answer.

It did not take me long to decide. I said, "I'm already in this up to my belt; I might as well go in up to my neck."

Upon accepting the post, however, I specified that if we won I would "ask nothing, expect nothing, accept nothing" in the way of emolument, of patronage, of high office, or high appointment from the new administration. If, for example, Magsaysay were elected and I were given back the ambassadorship in Washington which meant so much to me, the opposition could point to it and say, "Ah, there was the bribe!"

So I stipulated that I was to take nothing in the event of victory, a pledge I have scrupulously kept.

At this stage, the Presidential campaign of 1953 entered into its most historic phase.

It was our feeling and our conviction, Magsaysay's and mine, that every voter in the Philippines, every citizen, and every citizen's wife and dependent in the country should be spoken to directly, and have the privilege of hearing from the most qualified of spokesmen in the campaign what his rights were, what his obligations were, and what dangers he and his fellow citizens faced if he forgot his rights and failed in his obligations.

In other words, we would appeal directly to the people.

This was a chapter we and those with us in the coalition personally were prepared to write for the general history of man's struggle for freedom.

It must not be forgotten that the Nationalist-Democratic coalition, as headed by Magsaysay, had for its goal something which transcended mere political ambition and a desire to occupy the highest civil office in the land. This answer to the cry for a change in leadership came from the conviction that democracy in the Philippines was all but mortally ill, and that only a drastic reversal of trends of living and of governmental concepts could save it.

To carry this message to the large urban centers was relatively simple. It offered no greater complications than the procurement of permits for public meetings—often in itself a difficult task—buying time on the radio, and securing adequate press coverage. Therefore, it was no problem to deliver our message to the people of Manila and all the larger cities and towns. Our basic difficulty was to reach the overwhelming majority of the Filipino electorate who work and live out their lives in the rural regions, in the barrios distant from the *población*—the administrative and governmental and political center of their community, which in the majority of cases was under the control of officials favorable to the Quirino administration and hostile to our side.

Traveling between Manila and the important island areas of the archipelago was no problem with the splendid and ably operated air service afforded by the Philippine Airlines, and, for candidates who could afford chartered planes, with the network of landing fields left in the Philippines by the American liberating forces and expanded by a wise commercial air policy. It was only after we reached the provinces that the difficulties began.

Magsaysay was never averse to trouble. He went out to meet it. He was the first Filipino candidate to break through the old custom of addressing only large crowds in the provincial capitals and the commercial centers and to embark on a campaign of barrio-hopping. No village was too small, none too far away for his personal attention. By motor car, by jeep, by canoe or *vinta*—a small sail boat—by horse-drawn vehicle, and more often than not on foot, Magsaysay and his aides and the newspapermen assigned to follow this unique Presidential campaign launched on a hectic existence.

As national campaign manager of the coalition I felt it my duty to follow my leader into the hinterland. To explain all that we wanted to explain to the Filipino people we had to plunge beyond the ordinary metropolitan campaign areas and strike at the very roots of the popular vote—the deepest-grass growing roots of the Filipino population.

And so in that hot and rainy July of 1953, for the first time in our Filipino history, a Presidential candidate and his chief aide—his campaign manager—struck out by separate paths but with the same heartfelt purpose into the farthest, poorest, and loneliest regions of the Philippines.

Chapter XII

I HAD thought I knew the Philippines.

But what does the average New Yorker know of the Louisiana sharecropper, or the farmer tilling the stubborn soil of Oklahoma or northern Idaho?

While campaigning for Magsaysay I discovered my own country. For the first time I met with all strata of my own people.

I had known the surface Philippines all my life. I had seen the dead level of poverty, but from afar, as one looking through the wrong end of the telescope. In Manila, a center of civilization, one saw poverty, to be sure, but overbalancing it was the wonderful ease and the luxury. In Manila, as in all old cities, one is inured to squalor, and antiquity gives to poverty the protective coloration of the picturesque.

In my own town of Camiling I had seen something of poverty, but nothing compared to what I found farther inland.

During the war I had seen and personally experienced much of privation and suffering. But that had been wartime. It was not daily living.

Now for the next five months—July, August, September, October, November—spent in campaigning for Magsaysay,

I would eat, sleep, and live with and learn to know and understand the underprivileged people of the Philippines. We were taking the fight against Communism, both domestic and international, directly to the people, and we were received and welcomed by the people in the peasant huts of split bamboo poles standing above the mud or in little nipa homes where the earthen floors turned to muddy pools during the rainy season.

It seemed to me it was always raining.

In the rainy season which is summer you roll up your jeans, and take off your shoes, and are grateful for *zuecos*, the wooden clogs the peasants wear. And even worse than the rain was the dusty season when mouth, ears and nostrils, skin and hair, caked with grime. Speaking mostly out-of-doors, in the village plaza or in rented lots, I was always hoarse, always in fear that my voice would stop. Always wet and hot, or dry and hot, I wound up my speeches feeling the perspiration rolling down my legs and my voice hoarsening.

We flew from island to island, but on the trips into the interior we often rode on jolting oil trucks over the roads that were little better than jungle trails until they gave out completely. Sometimes we stopped at a bridge that had been washed out, or consisted merely of two bamboo poles, and leaving the truck we would trudge on for miles to our destination, or to a place where another truck waited to carry us on.

Slogging on foot over a muddy jungle trail in a steaming forest, one looked forward to journey's end. The trip could terminate only in the shack of a peasant, huddled on the floor under a leaky roof by the light of a guttering candle or small oil lamp, around a fire of carabao dung, sharing by use of the fingers the family dish of boiled rice with a sprinkle of salt, with the added delicacies perhaps of crude molasses or a dried salted fish, caught in the nearby river. For the night ahead there loomed the prospect of broken sleep in this crowded hut, where perhaps fourteen persons shared a room, not counting the family's meagre supply of livestock—pigs, goats, and a few chickens, stirring, snorting and rooting beneath one's head under the thin bamboo floor.

So the Filipino in the remote barrios had lived for centuries. So he was living still, in this year 1953.

I thought we had experienced misery in the tunnel of Corregidor and on Bataan. As I said before, that was war. It had prepared me for hardships, but nothing like this. Here were people who spent their lives in a perpetual tunnel.

I was with people who have never known what breakfast is, who work hard for two meals a day. I was with other people who have never known the luxury of two daily meals, who subsist on one. I was in huts where little bundles of odoriferous rags that were children lay on wet earth, with bloated bellies and skin diseases, dying without medical care.

I slept with these people, sharing their bedding. To carry with us our own blankets and pillows would have been as great an offense as to carry our own food. Poor as these people were, they had their pride, their natural courtesy. They wanted to give all they had. So I slept on pillows filthy and smelling, too tired to care. I dipped my hands in the common rice bowl.

In one hut we sat down with the family to a meal that consisted of the usual rice and a small boney fish. The grandmother of the family took mouthfuls of the fish, worked them with her toothless gums, and spat out the bones. The handful of chewed fish she gave to me. "This," she said, in the tenderest way, "I do only for my children."

What could I do?

We were among people who had never seen a newspaper, many, in fact, had never seen a bit of paper. With rueful memories of the Waldorf-Astoria, and armed with an elementary corncob stick to drive away the persistent pigs, I retired behind bamboo hedges. I learned to do without bathing and to wait for a river, or rain.

Before joining with Magsaysay I had made fun of his crusade for artesian wells. Now I saw for myself what wells could mean to these people, of whom eighty out of every hundred were drinking—as had their forefathers since time immemorial—the polluted water which made them ill. Bathing was done in rivers, the women washed the clothing white as snow in the rivers, and I marvelled, seeing the struggle at first hand, how their longing for cleanliness could survive.

Magsaysay was promising schools to the people, if he won. I visited the country schools. Some had roofs but no walls, others no roofs at all, and in many places the children studied sitting on the ground, or in the mud if it rained.

I thought back over the recent history of these our people. How I had worshiped our leaders and rejoiced in their forward planning! How I had idealized Quezon, the father of social justice! The minimum wage, the labor laws, the public health measures that had been hailed in turn as steps toward a higher civilization, all had been without meaning to the masses in the hinterland far from the centers of progress, these people living from hand to mouth and surviving on food that often was not fit for human consumption. The steps forward had meant nothing to them.

The only communication these countrymen of mine had with the government was when they went fearfully into the towns to pay their taxes, or when the soldiers came and took their chickens and eggs, and threatened them if they asked for payment.

This was government to these people. It gave nothing. It demanded all they had.

I was among people, untouched by the anti-Huk campaign, who were losing faith because there was nothing for them to hope for and trust in, and who would do anything for change. Everywhere, even in the remote barrios, I heard the echo of the cry that had opened the breach to Communism. "We want change—new names, new faces in our government."

All that I saw and heard made me fearful. This was the sort of talk that had carried Communism to power in other lands. I had no doubt it would be as effective here if there were no change, if Quirino stayed in power.

Quirino, safe in the dignity and comfort of Malacañan, was referring to our grassroots campaign as "vulgar." Not for him the handshaking with soil-stained farmers and their toil-worn wives and the kissing of their rag-wrapped babies. Magsaysay had no such inhibitions. He may have started into the hinterlands with the idea that a vote was a vote. But he knew now, and we all knew, that he was getting more than votes. He was winning these people to whom he had the courtesy to speak directly, not as a leader to his followers but as equal to equal, of his plans to alleviate their lot. The sadness of that lot this campaign tour had brought home to him, and to all of us who were following his way.

It required physical stamina to carry our message around the islands. Senator Cabili, that veteran campaigner, kept a wary eye on me, the tenderfoot and amateur. I knew he was watching me and I was determined not to show weakness. When he slept on a floor, I slept there; when he ate with fingers smeared in rice, molasses and fish, I ate the same food; when he pushed along wet trails, I was at his heels. Nothing in the war had been worse than this but I would not admit that to him. One day he looked at me and laughed. "I take off my hat to you, Rommy. You're a good trouper."

Once we were penetrating the most impassable region in Mindanao, along roads overgrown with jungle, when we were warned about the trail ahead. Other travelers had been ambushed, robbed, and killed there by bandits the day before. My friend and companion, Senator Cabili, told our anxious friends they were not to worry. "In fact," Senator Cabili added, "Romulo and I will outtalk the bandits and they will wind up by lending us money."

We went on, and nothing happened to us.

We were crossing one river when the motor of our boat died and we tossed about without food or water in that little boat for eighteen hours. Airplanes were out hunting us, but we did not know that.

It took us eight hours to cross Sarangani Bay by canoe. That was followed by four-and-a-half hours on a pony, then a two-hour walk through rice paddies steaming in the sun. On reaching the barrio I talked for three more hours, out-of-doors, in the sun.

All this to reach three hundred votes!

After such an ordeal I was anxious to know what impression I had made, and after the election I looked up the returns from that village. Two hundred and ninety-nine people had voted on our side. I still wonder what son-of-a-gun failed to appreciate my efforts!

On another trip to another far-off barrio we were crossing a bay when the motor of our boat stopped, started again, and died. Senator Cabili was philosophical. He slept. I fumed. We had not eaten breakfast and I was hungry. Finally the boatman got the motor started and we were off again. Senator Cabili woke up. He knew the country, and he realized the boatman had somehow turned the boat around. We were heading for the open sea. Cabili headed us back toward the island we were to visit. The motor promptly died again.

Finally the motor sputtered to life and we were off again, but towards the opposite shore, away from the island.

"Hey," I shouted to the boatman, "we're going the wrong way!"

He explained, "I know of a place on the other side where we can get some eggs."

"Eggs!" I spluttered as if I had been offered the most flagrant insult. We were carrying the message of democracy to the hinterlands, and this fellow was thinking of eggs! "People are waiting for us over there, and you are willing to keep them waiting to get something to eat. Turn the boat back!"

Senator Cabili opened one sardonic eye and closed it again. It was my first temper outburst of the campaign, and it was due solely to hunger.

As we neared the barrio we could see its one street stirring with life. Boys pushed out small boats and rowed out to meet us, cheering as they escorted us to shore. As I staggered wearily onto the beach women pressed forward to kiss our hands, then, in this tiny out-of-the-way barrio on this lonely island, like the Pied Piper, I was paraded down the single street and paraded back again. I was cheered and questioned and deferred to and paid every honor, given every courtesy, every show of deference, everything, in fact, except food. These people had come from their jungle farms to see and to question, and every hand had to be shaken at least twice and every question must be answered, and it was not until eleven o'clock at night that we sat down to our first meal of the day—boiled rice, heavy unleavened bread, and coffee that tasted like tea. They were giving us their best, but by that time I was too hungry to eat.

After the feast there were more questions to be answered. It was late before I crawled into my corner of the hut and tried to sleep, and could not. This was the end of a very long journey, and I was hungry, unbathed, and tired. I was looking forward to morning and to breakfast and for some reason the thought of the eggs I had scorned obsessed me. I became convinced that in the morning there would be eggs. I lay awake thinking of them—and scratching—and morning came and breakfast was the remains of the meal of the night before, only this time the rice and bread were cold, and only the coffee, weaker than ever, had been heated over.

While I was munching, a name popped into my mind. Somewhere on this forested island lived a man I had known in Manila—"Ponfi" Ponferrada, one of my best friends and staunch supporters. I recalled that he owned a plantation, and that he possessed livestock. Best of all, I had heard him speak of his modern conveniences.

The villagers sent a courier on ahead, and we were rushed off in a rickety truck with hard board seats that cracked the vertabrae at every jounce. We arrived at the plantation and were welcomed by my friend and his wife. A steer had been killed and was being barbecued, and meantime I took a bath, my first complete bath in two weeks, in a small room that had no lights, but a real tub. The water had been warmed in tin gasoline cans, and I lay back in the tub and groped for the soap in the dark and poured warm water over my blissful self with a coconut shell, and sniffed the smell of the barbecuing beef.

I knew then I was no trouper. But I didn't mind, I had succeeded in fooling Senator Cabili!

To many of us who were carrying the campaign of information into the remote islands the truism of Filipino hospitality had been a matter of academic knowledge. Now we learned it was very real indeed. There were hardships, but these were more than compensated for by the warmth of the welcome, and above all, the close attention our efforts drew from these, our people. We, who had all the cause for gratitude to them, were outdone in our gratitude by these simple citizens of the Philippines, who felt that they were learning from us, that we were bringing to them a message which vindicated their basic faith in their own rights which is their faith in democracy—the deep-rooted conviction of the man of the land that while man is born to labor, he is also born with the right to stand on his own feet, to seek opportunity for advancement for himself and his family, and, in that search for equality, to be afforded equal rights.

Never, in any of the hundreds of university classes I have faced, in any of the hundreds of audiences I have lectured before, have I encountered such wholehearted attention from old and young alike, such receptivity to ideas, such keenness of penetration to the heart of the matter as in the humble barrios of my country people.

Often I would find my audience waiting in the open plaza, sitting on the ground. Many had come from far away—in antique cars and trucks they came from two hundred miles away—and were hungry and tired, but they sat patiently, courteously, eager to hear. They wanted long speeches, and often if I began to speak in dialect their shouts would interrupt joyously, "English! English!" They wanted to hear the message of democracy in English, first because they understood English and were proud of the fact, and second because they knew I had carried the message of the Philippines to the United States in English, and they wanted to hear what America had heard.

There was so much they wanted to hear. There were so many questions about the government. So much had been promised them; so much had gone wrong. They were bursting to tell all that was in their hearts, but first, because courtesy is never wanting, they would hear all I had to say. Even then, the Filipino will understate what he feels. The American, with generations of authority behind him, can call the man in the White House any name he likes, but the Filipino is more courteous, or more repressed. Gradually and carefully he may admit, "Perhaps the man in power is doing his best, but I think there should be a change. . . ."

When Filipinos become Huks the traditions fall away; the courtesy is lost.

As I had said in my letter of resignation to Quirino, these people were weary and confused. Still, they were thoughtful. They wanted above all to do what was right.

I have known many people in many lands. Some have been given a great deal, and others less, but I have never seen people who possess so little as my countrymen, and who give so much. We were welcomed everywhere, we were given the best the people had, and if we were not careful, they would go into debt to give us better than they had. Again and again, everywhere we went I was impressed by their hospitality, their fight for cleanliness and a decent living, their unfailing politeness. This is inbred. No matter how hot the sun, a man removes his hat and he bows when you meet. Voices are never raised.

In the home, no matter how poor, the family live in gentleness and dignity. The family is the heart of life, a protective unit. The home is sacred. The father is patriarch of the clan and the mother matriarch, and the children, entering the house, kiss the hands of their elders, not in subservience, but in respect and love.

The children grow, but the respect and the communion remain. The family stays together. The son becomes a man, but there is no thought of his setting out on his own, not while there is work for him at home, and food for him there. He will remain with his family until he marries and starts a home of his own.

Perhaps he is fortunate enough to go as a student to Manila. He studies and learns much, and returns home for vacation, but not to flaunt his learning or strut his superiority before his elders. In the *tienda*, or village store, he may show off his brilliance, but not at home. There he gets into his farm clothes at once and is out feeding the pigs and goats and chickens, aware that his knowledge may save this farm for the family, and that his parents may have mortgaged it, and even sold the family carabao, to procure this education for him. For this he respects and reveres them, and he will not show them how much he has learned, and if they are wrong about some things, he will not let them know.

At six o'clock in the evening Angelus rings in the village church. In the rice fields the farmer stops his carabao and removes his hat and bows his head to pray. The woman washing clothing in the river crosses her wet arms over her breast and prays. The children stop their play and run to their grandfather, and group around him in the last rays of the sun; old and young, they pray together.

On this campaign for Magsaysay I saw on a wide scale the beautiful side of my country and its people.

As I have said, I have known people in many lands,

212

but on this campaign I found myself most of all deeply in love with my own people. Magsaysay had been right in saying that they have in them the capacity for greatness. Better still is their sweetness and gentleness that comes straight from the heart, which can be found only in a people essentially good.

The purely physical hardships of the campaign were not all we had to contend with. An administration which had insured easy living and comparative wealth for hundreds of thousands of its minor henchmen, not to mention the prerogatives of the higher echelons of the regime, rallied for a desperate defense under our heavy fire. The people were being wakened to the facts and the effect was noticeable. It was only to be expected, therefore, that despite pious utterances from Manila, every device of the rougher style of politics should be brought to bear against our campaign. Paid terrorists, well armed and often masquerading as "temporary police" with quasi-official status, were always present at any meetings held by Magsaysay and his campaigners. Sent ostensibly to "maintain order," in reality to foment disorder, they were a constant menace. President Quirino and his immediate lieutenants may have been sincere when they gave the promise of clean campaigning and clean elections, but obviously they could not control their henchmen in the interior, where we were thwarted and threatened at every turn.

This became standard procedure: I would go to the mayor for a permit to speak; he, holding a post owed to the Quirino forces, would refuse that permit. The open plaza was unfortunately "not available." (Someone else had been granted a permit several days before.) Or if a permit were granted, there would be no available hall. Owners of vacant lots were afraid to rent their sites, even for a night. So ways were closed to us by all the pressure of which a powerful regime is capable.

But nearly always we found a way.

In the town of Janiuay the mayor not only refused me a permit to speak but promised to run me out of town if I tried. We were denied the right to the plaza. An owner of the usual privately-owned lot was found and coerced into renting it to us. The meeting was a great success.

After it ended I made a beeline for the mayor's house. He opened the door in person. He was dressing for dinner and in the act of pulling on his trousers. When he saw me he dropped them. I explained with as much dignity as I could that I realized he had been within his rights to deny me permission to speak in the town's park. Still, since he was the town's foremost citizen and I a visitor, it was my duty to pay my respects!

We had a fine chat. I regretted I was unable to accept his invitation to dinner!

Our worst troubles were in provinces like western Negros (Negros Occidental) where the Liberal Party regime was so firmly entrenched that in preceding elections the opposition had not wasted time on a candidate for governor.

Bacolod, the heart of the Liberal stronghold in Negros, was the scene of an incident which proved to be one of the turning points in the campaign.

By this time our meetings had ceased to be political rallies and had turned in many cases into scenes of open scrimmage. The immense Magsaysay appeal had launched a trenchant counterattack against the rough-tactic politics of the regime. Time and again the invading forces of fully-armed goons, carrying enough firepower to stage another enemy invasion, were shoved back from Magsaysay's platforms by former resistance fighters who had never cowered before the Japanese and saw no reason why they should fear hired political gangsters. Now the goons were resorting to the trick of infiltrating the meetings and firing into the air dozens of bursts from the Thompson submachine guns with which they were amply provided.

It was like the old Japanese firecracker trick, designed to scare, not to kill, but it served its purpose, which was to instill fear and break up our meetings.

Under these conditions I went to Bacolod with the intention of holding a meeting in the Quirino stronghold.

The governor of the province, a Quirino man, issued warnings that I was not to be allowed to speak. It was important that a meeting be held in Bacolod. In the "dirty election" of 1949, mobs of hired gunmen had patrolled its streets, firing into the air to keep people inside their homes. As a result it was in Bacolod that "even the birds and bees" had voted for Quirino.

Before leaving for the place I was warned that the goons were rallying in full force, that I would not be allowed to speak, and that if I did I would not leave the place alive.

Of course the plaza was "not available," and the right

to speak in the plaza was refused. After much trouble a vacant lot was rented for the night.

Bacolod is a large town and boasts an airport. When I stepped from the plane a letter was handed me. It was in Spanish. *Get out of here as fast as you can. If you dare to speak we will shoot you.*

I drove to the house of a man who is every inch a gentleman, Dr. Antonio Lizores, my host. Another letter was sent there. *If you speak tonight in the lot you have rented you will go out of Bacolod feet first.*

My host begged me not to attempt the speech. But I have had experience with anonymous notes. I assured my friends, "If they really plan to shoot me, they wouldn't write about it. They would go ahead and shoot." Privately, I hoped this was the right deduction.

Another meeting was to be held early that evening at Cadiz, a town sixty miles away. I decided to drive there and open that meeting, then drive back to Bacolod to be the last speaker of the evening.

Four of us—two candidates, a driver, and myself—drove back from Cadiz that evening. In the dark the lights flared over a large tree felled across the road. We all got out to push it back and bullets sang around us. Someone yelled, "We're ambushed!"

Somehow we got into the car and around the tree. The glass of the car windows has been shattered but no one was hurt.

I returned to my host's house and had dinner. I did not want to alarm him so I did not mention what had happened, but I did not enjoy that meal. The radio was on, and the voices of the first speakers were coming from

216

the lot where I must soon appear, interrupted by the sounds of disturbance.

The gangsters were making so much noise, shooting in the air, yelling and giving catcalls, that no one could hear what the Senator-speakers were saying.

My host was urging me not to go. I must say I was not eager to attend the meeting. But the broadcast over the radio was a national hook-up, and people all over the Philippines were listening to these sounds of intimidation. A brutal fear was being sent over the air to all the islands.

Bacolod was a key city, here was a key situation. The fear would be strengthened if I did not appear that night. The Magsaysay constituents would not dare appear at the Bacolod polls at election time if this meeting failed.

So I went.

The crowd was remarkable for its size, considering the official attitude to our cause and the amount of intimidation being used. At least twenty thousand people were standing in the open air, trying to hear a Senator whose speech was being interrupted by loud catcalls. When I reached the edge of the crowd a tremendous cheer drowned out the jeers; the people had given up hope of my arrival. I was picked up and tilted onto shoulders and rushed to the platform, and then and there, blinking against the blinding lights, I surveyed the crowd. Nearly all the faces were welcoming, and so friendly, but there was also the uneasiness of fear, and it was not hard to see why. I am not a brave man, and with quivering knees and a quaking heart I counted, scattered at strategic points in the crowd, between twenty-five or thirty men wearing brown shirts, looking in fact like Hitler men, and gripping the business end of Tommyguns, while on the stage, pressing closely about to protect me, were about ten members of the local constabulary.

Instantly I felt that the police, not the gunmen, were the more dangerous, because the gunmen would aim for me while the constabulary shooting back would have to aim at the gunmen scattered through the crowd. The result would be massacre.

I asked the sergeant in charge to order the men off the platform. They moved back, and I thought they left.

The Senator finished his speech amid many interruptions and I was introduced. As I took my place before the loud-speaker I glanced around. Four of the constabulary were still on the platform. I spoke my first words directly into the microphone:

"I don't want these soldiers up here. Ask them to leave the platform. I don't need any protection."

After they had taken new positions behind the platform, I began to speak. I talked to the people of Bacolod. I told them how, before and after arriving in their town, I had been threatened, but I had remembered Bataan and Corregidor when we had all fought together for democracy, and that since arriving in Bacolod I had seen no signs of the democracy we had fought for. Then I pointed one at a time to the brown-shirted men with the Tommyguns.

"You!" I said, "And you! Leave this meeting. You have no business here."

Anger makes one temporarily brave. I knew that at any moment I might turn tail and run for my life. No one

218

knew if these hoodlums were bluffing. But I had to find out.

This was not only a crisis in the fight for democracy. It was a golden opportunity to expose a brutal bluff and calm down an intimidated people. The microphone before me was open to all the Philippines. Every word and every sound made by me or by the crowd before me would be heard by our entire nation. Such an opportunity might never come again.

So I stood my ground, while the goons raised their guns one by one and cocked them slowly, with menacing looks leveled over the barrels. I carried the mike forward, to the very edge of the platform. Again I ordered the goons to leave.

Some fired into the air in answer, but a few of the bullets seemed very close. Screams and shouts came from every side over the rattle of the guns. To say that I was frightened is the understatement of the year. But I heard myself shouting in a voice louder than any other.

I was shouting to the goons, "Shoot if you have to, but shoot me!" Then to the people, "Don't run! Keep your ground! These cowards don't dare fire." And again to the hoodlums, "Go ahead if you dare, shoot me!"

And there was silence on the field. All over the islands, wherever radios exist, there was nothing then but silence. The gangsters were silent, and that silence, those who listened over the air told me later, held the greatest intensity of the night and it was felt in every remote corner of the Philippines. Not another shot was fired. I waited. No one moved. Nothing happened. Then I spoke, to all listening everywhere:

"People of the Philippines, do you hear this? They don't dare shoot! Don't be afraid any more. Go out on election day. Vote!"

I stood watching the gunmen slink one by one out of the crowd, and then I made the speech of my life. By the time I finished the crowd was enormous.

People who had not dared attend, but who had been listening over the radio, had come running.

As soon as I returned to my host's house there was a telephone call from Virginia in Manila. My wife had been listening. Her voice shook, but she made a joke of things. "Do you have to be so brave? Don't forget you have a family." And a wire came from a Manila editor: "Wonderful, but don't do it too often."

Newspapers in the Philippines and the United States praised the "act of courage." It had nothing to do with courage. Courage is spontaneous. This was not. I had thought it all out and had prepared for it, and I had been frightened every moment. When I was carried onto the platform on those shoulders I was shaking so I could hardly hold on. When I carried the microphone to the platform's edge my knees were wobbling so hard I had to use it as a crutch. But out of some hidden resource I marshaled enough strength to carry me through and I know that given the same circumstances, I would be able to do it again.

The incident at Bacolod was a windfall to the newspapers. It was given editorial comment throughout the Philippines, and carried by news agencies all over the United States. It focused attention on the goon tactics being used against the Magsaysay campaign.

The result was a surge of interest as American publishers saw a story in the making, and a convergence on Manila of two score of the ablest American correspondents.

It is true that most of these were trained reporters of war who came down from the Korea battlefields in the expectation of seeing an election that would actually be another war. But by the time they arrived the Filipinos had been so aroused by the exposure of terrorism that the terrorists had gone underground. Even the highest levels of the administration had wakened to the conclusion that rough stuff in politics was a thing of the past. The results gave additional force to the already all but uncontrollable popular swing toward Magsaysay.

It is to the credit of President Quirino and his immediate subordinates that the foreign correspondents were afforded every facility for travel and observation. Needless to say, none of their dispatches was censored, since there is no censorship in the Philippines.

Attempts to win the election by any means did not cease. Plans were laid for wholesale fraud at the polls, after the ballot-counting. The Quirino administration continued to transfer to key election centers the provincial treasurers and provincial constabulary commanders known for their allegiance to the regime; for in the Philippines, it is the provincial treasurer who controls the return of the ballot boxes, and the commander who controls the constabulary troops whose duty it is to guard the polls.

In the "clean election" of 1951, Magsaysay had called on the troops to insure safety to voters and an honest ballot.

Now the people became apprehensive that Quirino might, as Commander-in-Chief, call on the uniformed men to insure his own re-election. If this happened, a civil war would result. But the armed forces stood loyally by their individual oath of allegiance to uphold the Constitution of the Philippines, including the right to a free election. Our soldiers protected the people in that right and proved further that in times of crisis the people could depend on them.

The Filipinos—and the world—had wakened to danger. Someone in the lower echelons of the regime in power had gone too far, and the people, grasping the full significance of the struggle to preserve their way of life, were thoroughly aroused.

It is, I believe, partly due to this awakening that the election when it took place was one of the cleanest and most orderly ever held in the Philippines.

Chapter XIII

THREE million Filipinos, from city, barrio, and farm, from factory and mine, from school and store, rolled Ramón Magsaysay into the Presidency on November 10, 1953, on a tide that proved irresistible.

There was no violence on the scale expected, nor anything near it. In Cavite, where political passions normally run at fever heat, nine persons were killed in a shooting affray which bore a closer resemblance to an ancient vendetta than to a political clash. The Chicago *Tribune* in commenting on this incident noted trenchantly in an editorial that the casualty list of nine in an election where some five million voted was "slightly under par for Kentucky."

Unprecedentedly for an election campaign in the Philippines, this one had organized within seven months the greatest mobilization of the citizenry in our political history. Only seven months before, "The Guy," as Magsaysay was affectionately known, had announced his intention to run against organized power. The Filipinos had not only proven themselves aware of the great issue involved, but they had rallied to numerous active "movements," sparked and promoted by citizens who had come to believe that the obligation of a citizen transcends the mere act of marking and depositing a ballot.

His first direct supporters, including men who had fought at his side against the Japanese, had sparked the formation of the "Magsaysay for President Movement." The young and virile Ramón Magsaysay, with his splendid fighting record, had naturally made his strongest appeal to the youth. His personality, intensely Filipino in every way, appealed to all. Within a matter of weeks the whole archipelago, from the Bashi Channel to the Sulu Sea, was dotted with MPM Clubs. The women played almost as decisive a role, and in their Women's Magsaysay for President Movement, led by Mrs. Pacita Madrigal Warns, soon rivaled the stronger sex in the extent and intensity of their campaigning. The Namfrel (National Movement for Free Elections, organized by public-spirited civic leaders before the 1951 elections, when Magsaysay had first emerged as defender of the people's right to freedom in elections) lent the weight of its prestige to such an extent that the Liberal Party chieftains branded it as an opposition movement. The press was overwhelmingly for a clean and fair election. The radio, in all its elements, and this included the government-owned and -operated stations, gave free access where it did not openly support us.

Senator Laurel had aided when he yielded the chance for the candidacy. He might have had the nomination, and with an even better chance of ultimate victory, since at the time of the Nationalist Convention he was far better known than Magsaysay.

Victory had been assured when we halted the three-cornered race and joined the Democratic to the Nationalist Party in the coalition.

All these factors contributed the landslide vote for Magsaysay, but, of course, the major factor was the man's dynamic and convincing personality and his record for courage and honesty, which had won the love and trust of the Filipino people.

He was perfectly confident on that Tuesday, our election day. So, we were told, was Quirino. A few hours of the early returns showed how misplaced was Quirino's confidence.

The Philippine press and radio performed a major miracle and for the first time the results of the election were made known in Manila on Wednesday, November 11. So decisive were the earliest reports that Speaker Eugenio Perez, President of the Liberal Party, conceded the election that very day.

Two days later, President Quirino followed suit.

Magsaysay was victor in what he has described correctly as "the most truly democratic election ever held in Asia."

He had paved the way for this victory when he gave the Filipinos their "clean election" of 1951.

Now he held the fruits of that victory. Five million two hundred thousand Filipinos, women and men, had registered for this free election. Of these more than three million had voted for Magsaysay.

Philippine democracy had risen from its sickbed, revitalized and all but whole.

Still there was a vestige of anxiety left in the minds of some of our friends overseas, and, if the truth be told, of some of our compatriots at home. Bearing in mind the flood of political excoriation, the bitterness of the campaign, the scars it must have left, and the fact that one million five hundred thousand Filipinos had voted staunchly for Quirino, the question remained: could Magsaysay assume the leadership of the people in an atmosphere of peace, or would there be tension and potential conflict?

The question was complicated by the opening measures taken by the President-elect. Directly after his election Magsaysay withdrew from the public eye. Closeted with friends and trusted advisers he began plotting his course for a clean-up of the government and for the carrying out of his most important election pledges. He appointed committees to inquire into every phase of governmental activity, from finances to the administration of justice. His investigators probed into the workings of the so-called government corporations, through which the government controlled procurement and distribution of vital commodities, managed public services, and sought to handle the problem of providing for the landless masses.

When these investigators brought out the facts and situations which demonstrated the shaky position of the whole government, the resentments and animosities bred by the bitter campaign were given new life and new point.

During these weeks of pre-inaugural seclusion the President-to-be was mapping the future of the Philippines.

More than half a million people turned out to see Magsaysay inaugurated on the Luneta at high noon of December 30. The inauguration of "The Guy" was marked with "timetable precision," "austerity," and "simplicity."

There had been some unease as to post-election repercussions. It proved groundless. As the grandstands filled, Ramón Magsaysay with his aides and an escort of honor drove to Malacañan Palace. Outgoing President Quirino received him in his study, embraced his young successor, and insisted that the new President try sitting in his official desk chair "for size." The meeting was symbolical of the newly-won unity of the people. The two left the Palace with their arms over each other's shoulders and, escorted by cavalry, drove slowly to the Luneta.

President Quirino was reported to have been reluctant to take this ride because he feared the crowds along the route might jeer him. But the slow progress of the Presidential car was made to resounding cheers, from the Palace to the grandstand on the Luneta.

The two Presidents left the car together and received the Presidential salute of twenty-one guns as army bands played the greetings for a commander-in-chief and our national anthem. Then they shook hands, ex-President Quirino returned to the car, and, escorted by his own guard of honor and cheered to the echo on every side, he drove away to his little farm in Novaliches—perhaps to contemplate the twists and turns of history. His stalwart successor, stripped of all the carefully prearranged security measures, was carried to the platform on the shoulders of his people.

This was the highest demonstration—as far as political struggle was concerned—of political maturity. The hand of good will was extended from either side. No adherents of the defeated party were forced to flee the country. No lists of proscription were issued. There were no exiles, no coups, no reprisals—nothing but the enthusiasm and pride of a people united in the flame of political conflict.

The inaugural address of the new President was only twenty minutes long, but every word carried weight. A tall, powerful, essentially Asian figure, Magsaysay towered over many on the platform, wearing the simple attire the majority of his listeners wore—a plain *barong-tagalog*, or native shirt, and gray trousers.

In that brief talk he pledged his program: social justice for all; land for the landless; protection of individual rights and the welfare of the common man; and selfless service in the interests of the people.

"We will run this government by deeds, not speeches," promised Magsaysay.

He voiced then, and stressed later in his State of the Nation message to Congress on January 25, 1954, his deep concern for the well-being of the farmer. "There are too many laws in too many books," he said. And he pointed out that what was needed was a "single, concise and easily understood farm tenancy code."

Then, undaunted by the formidable task before him of raising a nation's standard of living through accelerated economic development, he exclaimed, "For this young and vigorous nation of ours, nothing is impossible!"

Many millions of Filipinos, listening on the Luneta or in their homes, knew that the very fact that President Magsaysay had been given the power to stand on that platform and voice such words proved they were true.

Magsaysay made, and kept, his pledge of austerity. That night a long-standing tradition was broken. No inaugural ball was held at Malacañan. Instead, the Magsaysays dined *en famille* in the Palace; their guests were five intimate friends.

On January 1, the first day of the New Year and Magsaysay's first day in office, the President had the doors of Malacañan thrown open for the people, so that those "who own this place, can see what it looks like." He said that Malacañan, the seat of centuries of regal splendor, would be known henceforth as Malacañang, to conform with the native pronunciation. As for himself, he preferred being addressed plainly as "Mr. Magsaysay" instead of the formal "Mr. President."

Subsequently, he instructed Malacañang officials to charge to his salary all expenses incurred by his personal guests at the Palace, or on board the Presidential yacht, the *Pagasa,* or in the President's out-of-town residence, such as the Guest House at Baguio.

He had large problems to solve for a new and vigorous democracy. One required immediate attention: the reasons behind the threatened decay of that democracy.

He had learned the answer in his fight against the Communists. Graft, corruption in high places, fraudulent elections, nepotism had spawned the Red brigades. He proceeded to take the lid off government affairs and let the people see how they worked. He promised that his administration's policy with officials charged with corruption would be "prosecution, not persecution."

By declaring his own personal assets, he set the example for government officials and employees to do the same; he was, in effect, implementing the "morality in government" injunction of his State of the Nation message. He ordered his Cabinet members to give up their teaching jobs and other sidelines so that they could devote full attention to their departments. He announced that all gifts made to himself or to his family, except those given by a few old and intimate friends, would be turned over to charity; this led to the establishment of what is now known as the "Ramón Magsaysay Welfare Fund."

The new President put into immediate effect his plan to make unannounced and surprise visits to various parts of the country, explaining that he wanted to see living conditions as they were from day to day, not "dressed up" for his benefit as they would be if his visits were known beforehand. Also, he wanted to spare government officials and the people the burden and expense of preparing elaborate receptions. His only purpose in making these provincial trips was to get work done, which was best accomplished without fanfare.

In his first three months in office, Magsaysay visited many villages and towns, including many remote and inaccessible communities where no President had ever set foot before. He conferred with local officials and talked with the people, and his first questions were invariably about the people: Did they have artesian wells? Were they afflicted with disease? Were there adequate schools for the children? Did they have good roads and a steady means of earning a livelihood?

So he studied at first hand the problems and needs of each locality, including the enforcement of the laws and the ways in which the government could help solve the difficulties.

Speaking before a huge throng at the Obando Community Plaza on February 11, Magsaysay said that it was his desire to improve conditions for all the Filipino people, particularly those living in the rural areas. He made active demonstration of this in many towns, such as in Obando, and in San Luis, Pampanga, when he approved on the spot the release of funds to improve the waterworks systems of the barrios.

No previous President had noted or cared if the people had pure water or not. Magsaysay saw and felt with the eyes and heart of the common man, and he was the first to take an interest. Only twenty per cent of the Filipinos were drinking potable water; the other eighty per cent drank it polluted.

Magsaysay made a promise: "An artesian well for every barrio!" Three hundred million pesos, which we did not have, were needed for this project; it would be a cheap price to pay for the health of a nation.

From January 1, Magsaysay's first day in office, to February 15, sixty artesian wells were constructed in provinces, municipalities, and barrios. Popular support for the undertaking was launched through the Liberty Wells Association, created by public-spirited citizens as a tribute to President Magsaysay. By March 10 it had received contributions and pledges amounting to almost $500,000. The slogan of the association is an ancient Chinese proverb: "God will bless those who dig wells, build bridges and construct roads."

In the United States, two good friends of the Philippines, ex-Ambassador Myron Cowen and Major General Leland Hobbs, organized an association called the Committee for Philippine Action for Development, Reconstruction and Education (COMPADRE) to help collect funds for Magsaysay's artesian well project.

To channel into constructive outlets the explosive unrest that had been generated in the country, Magsaysay formulated and put into effect, on March 21, 1954, a five-year-plan of economic and social development, to be based on our own national resources.

This plan for the future was designed to raise living standards for the Filipinos as rapidly as democratic processes and the inertia of centuries would allow. It was a frontal attack on poverty, hunger, and disease—the ancient enemies of economic and social progress in such under-developed countries as the Philippines.

He listed as its most important aims the re-establishment of the people's confidence in the government, reduction of unemployment, increase of production, improvement of living conditions in the barrios, and the destruction of the last vestiges of the Communist-led Hukbalahap movement.

The Philippines was suffering from disadvantages common to all underdeveloped countries—meagerness of domestic savings, unstable income from primary products, and an inadequacy of investment capital and technical know-how.

The plan, therefore, was a modest one, which stressed the role of private Filipino enterprise and tempered the unrealistic dream of inpourings of riches from international or other external sources. There could be no more wild dreams. We had been taught a frightening lesson in reality in the Philippines, and like the Americans after the "big crash" of 1929, we had to realize that from this time on we would have to stand on our own feet and any future we had must be of our own making.

Foremost among the many problems facing our under-developed land was the need to find more jobs. To this end the plan led to the establishment of power, communication, transport and credit services, and new basic industries, thereby creating in the first year 260,000 new jobs, and 360,000 each year thereafter.

A two-hundred-million-peso public-works program was launched, with an initial fifty million pesos to be spent the first year. The plan called for the concrete surfacing of five of the country's vital highway networks and for the improvement and construction of roads, streets, and bridges. Later, over fifteen million pesos was released for this fund.

Plans began for the construction of new schools.

The land reform movement which had held Magsaysay's deep personal interest, and which had been the cause of his first serious disagreement with the Quirino regime, was an important part of the general plan for economic development. With all the resources of the government behind it, the movement included the opening of new settlements for the landless, fair land-reform laws, methods for increasing productivity in agriculture, rural co-operatives, flood control and multi-purpose river projects, extensive courses for farmers, more effective marketing facilities, and diversification of the economy through the creation of light industries based on local materials.

The total first-year investment contemplated under the five-year-plan is only 631,000,000 pesos, or $315,500,000. It will levy a tax to the limit of our public and private resources. Whatever private savings and domestic capital exist must be tapped in support of the plan; more than a third will have to come from bank loans and private borrowing. The Executive Secretary of the United Nations Economic Commission for Asia and the Far East has pointed out the Asian dilemma: "To curtail the economic development program or to incur budgetary deficit." Despite that threat, our plan for the future has all our hopes. Against it are the hazards of shifting market prices and changes in trade. Our need from the outside is the guarantee of stable returns, international assistance in financing, and the good will of the world.

Balancing these in support of the plan is the Filipino desire for a better and safer life, and our dream of independence. That dream is now active. Any threat to it now must come, not from inside the Philippines, but from the outside, by invasion.

The human dream ends with this—a family together at sundown, fed, sheltered, without fear. It was kept in mind in outlining the five-year plan.

The clean-up in government played a strong role in the plan. Graft, nepotism, preference in government are the filth that Communism feeds upon. Magsaysay said pointedly: "Our people in government have not been completely aroused out of their apathy. Many are still as listless, indifferent and inefficient as before. They don't seem to realize that a change has come—that now they are expected to render their utmost service with missionary zeal and personal sacrifice."

Those who failed to realize this met with unpleasant surprises. The President demanded the resignation of a director of the bureau of private schools who had failed to act quickly to stop the progress of veritable diploma mills; he suspended a mayor in Negros Occidental who was indicted in court on four counts of falsification of public documents; and he dismissed a foreign-affairs officer who had been negligent.

With the full weight of authority he launched the final all-out attack on the remaining Communist Huks. It was a campaign of justice tempered with mercy, the same policy he had maintained as Secretary of Defense.

He began by throwing the government's forces against the die-hard Huks, while at the same time enlarging his program to raise living conditions in the barrios and developing the "land for the landless" program—two movements calculated to expose the emptiness of the Red propaganda. Moreover, he left the door open to individual surrenders by the Huk rank and file, with the condition that those facing charges must stand trial, while those without criminal records would be given an opportunity to live peaceful and productive lives.

Ten days after becoming President, Magsaysay extended executive pardons to twenty-five prisoners lodged in the Masbate provincial jail and ordered their immediate resettlement on Burias Island.

He had the provincial commander there allocate six hectares of land to each prisoner and help him settle. Food and clothing were provided for the men and their families.

He had personally interviewed these prisoners. He said of them: "These people were starving. Their families were hungry. All they knew was that they had to have something to eat. These people are the most inflammable material for the spread of Communism in our country!"

On that same January tenth that these prisoners were set free, Magsaysay inspected the progress of a reclamation project involving several thousand hectares of rich rice lands in San Luis, Pampanga, the home town of the Huk leader Luis Taruc. This project had been abandoned for eight years due to dissident activities. Pampanga was the last stronghold of the Huks. Taruc was still hiding somewhere in the province.

President Magsaysay called upon the army to send engineer task forces to clear the barrios and build roads in order to encourage tenant-farmers-turned-Huk to return to their homes. The soldiers worked day and night, stringing wires, digging artesian wells, and clearing the barrios of treacherous *talahib* growths.

Seventeen days later, Lieutenant General Jesus Vargas, AFP Chief of Staff, announced that the reclamation project in San Luis was almost finished and that he expected a turnover of 3,200 hectares of land to LASEDECO for redistribution to the landless.

It was democracy's final offer to the disbelieving.

The majority of the last of the Huks were the embittered and disillusioned, and these as they took faith again came down to the barrios bringing their guns, turning them in, along with all the nirvana promises of Communism, for the actuality of real land under one's feet and the chance at normal freedom.

Those who continued to hide found their waistlines and their chances of survival slimming. The people, recharged with democratic fervor and holding new faith in their government and in Magsaysay, no longer continued to give the Huks food or to help hide them when the soldiers came. Faced with destitution or capture, many more rebels gave in.

On May 17, 1954, Huk-Supremo Luis Taruc, who since 1945 had been the Communist leader of the Hukbalahap rebels and the symbol of Red rebellion in the Philippines, came alone out of a morass in Pampanga and surrendered. For almost a decade he had kept the Philippines in constant threat of revolution. A price of fifty thousand dollars had been on his head. Now he was a thin, tired, worn-looking ex-rebel, cut away on every side from the cause that had failed him, and glad to give in.

Taruc's surrender was a final triumph for Democracy, and for President Magsaysay. Many times since becoming President, Magsaysay had tried to negotiate with Taruc and bring him to the point of surrender. Something had always gone wrong. But Taruc had found himself at journey's end, a stray fox hiding out in the Candaba swamp in the province of Pampanga, with his followers killed or captured or having deserted in favor of the democratic side. He who had whipped up the masses was now ignored by the masses. There was no more discontent on which he could feed the people. They would no longer protect him. The army had him surrounded. Rather than be killed, Taruc surrendered.

As I write this, Taruc has received a sentence of twelve years for rebellion, a sentence that has been protested as too lenient by President Magsaysay. The charge of rebellion covers and supersedes all other crimes, such as pillage and murder. The President holds that Taruc should be tried individually on each of these grounds, and as a result the Department of Justice has ordered the prosecuting fiscal to file new charges that cannot be considered double jeopardy against Taruc. Whatever the outcome, it is not the results of his trial but the surrender of Taruc that is the victory.

His surrender marked the final collapse of internal subversion in the Philippines.

A small percentage of Huks are still hiding in the hills. Among these are some who were felons under long sentence, or prisoners awaiting trial who were set free by the Japanese when Japan invaded. These do not wish to stand trial. They remain at large.

At present, Communism in the Philippines has shrunk to less than two thousand outlaw Huks, with a remainder of Huk sympathizers estimated at thirty-two thousand. This is not too high a percentage, out of a population of nearly twenty-one million!

Democracy had won over Communism less by armed force than by the emotional pressure exerted by a united nation. Material, moral, and spiritual aid from America helped the Filipino people in their fight for freedom. From their own inner resources they drew the conviction that assured victory. That conviction was fostered and directed by a man with an understanding of the human dream.

Magsaysay has said: "Communism is an idea you cannot kill with sword or gun. When a man with an empty belly works in a rice paddy on land which is not his, always in debt and with his children hungry—when a man in that position hears someone say, 'Land belongs to the man who works it, come to us and we will give it to you,' then something happens to that man. It is as if a cool wind blew through a hell on earth."

The fight for complete democracy is never ending, no matter how free the land. Our conflict in the Philippines is not completely over. But the beacon light of democracy that came perilously close to being totally extinguished has been rekindled, and it has brightened the face of Asia.

It flared to life with the free election that made Ramón Magsaysay President of the Philippines. That was far from being a merely domestic victory. It engendered new faith in sections of Asia where the people were wearied by war, poverty, and oppression, and where millions were ready to bend under the hammer-and-sickle. American press response to our election warmed our hearts, but even more satisfying has been the renewal of enthusiasm for democracy in other parts of Asia than our own.

The Philippines were to be "Democracy's show window" in the Orient.

That window looks two ways. Geographically and spiritually, the Philippines lie halfway between America and the Far East. We can see both sides. We saw what Communism had done in neighboring lands and denied it the right to take over ours. We have refused diplomatic relations with Russia. The Red ideal has no place in our show window. It took tremendous effort on our part, but the window shines.

On March 10, 1954, President Magsaysay issued a statement clarifying our foreign policy with reference to Asia.

"The Philippine Government," he said, "stands for the right of self-determination and independence of all Asian nations; for closer cultural and economic relations and mutual cooperation with freedom-loving Asian countries as a group and within the framework of the Charter of the United Nations; and for the proposition that a return to colonialism, of which the last vestiges are now disappearing from Asia, shall not be tolerated in any form."

In an earlier statement, on February 22, he had said he saw nothing incompatible between friendship and sympathy for Asian neighbors and the continuation of a cordial relationship with the United States. He said then, "There is no conflict of principles, ideals or methods between those concepts."

No matter what happens next to our world, to us in the Philippines, or to our President Magsaysay, we can never forget that in a dark and dangerous time he served as the symbol of democracy to the Far East. Magsaysay had been in the forefront of four great Filipino struggles that were of importance to all Asia, which is to say, to the whole world: the fight against Japanese invasion, the fight against Communist domination, the effort to raise living standards for a people, and the fight for clean democratic government.

He gave the world its first locally achieved victory over international Communism. He not only subdued the Huks; he rehabilitated. He drove fear and distrust from the country—and with the lifting of fear the economic situation improved; he healed the rift in a people that had been skilfully divided by the weight of Red propaganda; he helped restore the Republic and prevented our slipping into chaos.

To the Filipinos, Ramón Magsaysay is our Abraham Lincoln, our leader risen from and for the masses. To the rest of Asia he has assumed even larger stature. There are millions in areas dark with oppression who are beginning to look to Magsaysay as the true Asian, the new leader, who may yet emerge as the new and true leader of all Asia.

The start and advance of the five-year plan I watched from the other side of the world. I did not attend the Magsaysay inauguration. I had pledged myself, if he won, to accept no titles, no honors. Three days after his election I returned to the United States to make a new beginning and a new living. I told our new President I would serve my country in Washington, without portfolio or title and without salary. That is why I spend most of my time in Washington, no longer representative of the Philippines in the United States, but as the President's special, personal, unsalaried envoy.

Up to the time I write, since returning from the Philippines I have spoken in nearly six-hundred American cities.

Once before, in 1942 after Corregidor fell, I toured the United States and spoke to Americans of the danger in the Pacific. I had been sent to the United States by General Douglas MacArthur to alert America. I talked then to hundreds of thousands of Americans of the Filipino fight to hold the Philippines to the side of democracy. The battle word then was: "Remember Bataan!"

Again, twelve years later, I am back in the United States on the same desperate mission, calling attention once more to the struggle in the Pacific where democracy is going from defeat to defeat, and where its strength, its prestige, and its very security are steadily weakening

241

under the onslaught of an enemy far greater and more determined on destruction than was Japan.

Again I am reporting to Americans the Filipinos' continuing fight to hold the democratic lines against aggression, giving, as an example of hope and courage, our own victory over Communism inside the Philippines.

There are times I meet with an American who says, "But what has all that fighting over there to do with *me*? 'Asia for the Asians!' What have I to do with anything that concerns the other side of the Pacific?"

For this American I have but one answer. "Take a look at the map, my friend!"

Chapter XIV

VIEWED from the Pacific side the world seems to fall in half like a split apple: rimming one side is Asia, and the other, America. Study the map of Asia, its red-stained areas and those that are still free, and it is easy to see that the free world's line of defense lies on Asia's side of the Pacific.

The pattern of Soviet conquest is very clear. The chain of defense is equally so. Starting at the Aleutians, it is the holding line between American freedom and Soviet power.

Trace it southward on the map, through Japan, Korea, Formosa, Okinawa, Guam, and the Philippines. The Philippines are as a scattering of pinpoints. The United States is much larger and Russia many times larger—large enough to swallow up the world.

Russia is doing just that. Already, it has swallowed up two-thirds of our world.

And still, our pinpoint archipelago has held the line against Communism. Not once, but twice has the Philippines resisted nations bent on conquest, and each time succeeded in upsetting the time schedules set by aggressors far stronger and better-armed: Japan and Russia.

The march of conquest has twice led southward, following the Pacific line of defense. Japan, bent on world conquest, was the first to attempt to break the chain, link by link, starting in China. From China the conquerors could go north and south, through Japan and then Formosa, down to the Philippines. After the Philippines the way would be open to Australia and New Zealand—the last links in the semicircle that shields the American hemisphere.

That chain can hold only as long as its weakest link can hold. While we cannot say which is the weakest link, we do know that in all of Southeast Asia the Philippines is America's only proven ally—America's only proven friend. Aiming to make its conquest doubly certain, Japan struck at the strongest link, the Philippines, thus revealing its blueprint of conquest. Though conquered we continued to fight, and eventually saw the defeat of Japan. Then, from the same direction, we were threatened again.

Russia took over the Japanese blueprint of conquest, following it at every step. Since the ultimate objective of Soviet Communism is world domination, the Communists, too, first invaded China. Having done this, they struck through Korea. But there they were halted and pushed back.

Remember, however, that the Japanese, six months before Pearl Harbor, occupied Indochina. They were aware of the strategic value of the territory; they knew that from there they could branch out in every direction for further conquests.

But of even greater importance is the fact that Indochina is the rice bowl of Southeast Asia. In the Philippines before the war we imported much rice from Saigon. Just as Japan had needed rice for its soldiers and its citizens, so Communist China now needs rice to feed its hungry people. To succeed in China, the Communists must have rice. If the Communists can control Indochina and help fill the millions of empty Chinese stomachs, they can control not only China, but other Asian countries where hunger is Communism's strong ally.

Japan tried to accomplish this, and failed. Russia, following the Japanese blueprint in every detail, is determined not to fail.

Japan tried to integrate China, Manchuria, and Korea into the Japanese economy, and failed. Russia is assembling the pattern now, and achieving victory after victory. North Korea, the industrial zone of Korea, has been conquered. Manchuria, next on the blueprint, is the industrial zone of China.

The basic strategy of Soviet Russia now is to integrate Manchuria, the industrial zone of China, and North Korea, the industrial zone of Korea, with Soviet economy. Beyond these lie Japan, Formosa, and the Philippines. If Russia succeeds, the challenge to America's industrial power will be very serious indeed.

The United Nations stopped the Communists in Korea, so they went into Indochina.

The importance of Korea was that it revealed to the world the blueprint of Communism. It was Russia's first decisive action after the conquest of China. It showed the way Russian aggression has followed Japan's at every step. The pattern is still incomplete, still developing, yet it follows irrevocably the objective outlined by Nikolai Lenin when he wrote: "The road to London and Paris is through Peiping and Calcutta." This means Russia plans to conquer Asia first, then Europe, then America. "And tomorrow the world."

Japan had used brute force. Russia, employing typically Communistic tactics in its attempt to conquer the Philippines, also struck energetically, but from within, using the softening-up process that prepares the ground for the seeds of Communism. Unlike Japan, Russia had help from within the Philippines, where the Communist ally inside the gates was our people's loss of faith in the government.

Under the tutelage of Communist leaders, the Huks were softening up the Philippines so that after Korea was conquered, the Philippines would be ripe and ready to fall.

But instead of succumbing, we upset the time schedule of Soviet aggression. When we crushed the Huk rebellion in the Philippines we helped to arrest the forward march of the Soviet to world supremacy—halfway between Russia and the American mainland. Russia's infiltration tactics succeeded elsewhere, but not in the Philippines.

The blueprint of aggression was stopped for the second time in the Philippines. The Communists had failed to count on one obstacle, which is the Filipino's passion for freedom.

In the crisis, it was not so much the force of arms that helped us hold the line. It was, rather, the restoration of faith in our own government, the realization that part of the Communist plan for world conquest was the encouragement and support of the Huk uprising, the turning of brother against brother, the weakening of the government and of the people's faith in the government, that the Communists might take over. They carried out this plan up to the last move.

The plan was to bring about the collapse of the Philippines through internal dissension rather than by military attack. We were being pushed relentlessly from political conflict into civil war, and then into revolution. That was the way the Communists were conquering in other parts of Asia.

It almost worked. Filipino was turned against Filipino as Chinese had been turned against Chinese, Korean against Korean, Greek against Greek. That is the Soviet strategy, the way Russia wins. Russia has developed to the nth degree the success formula of all despots: "Divide and rule."

In a succession of bloodless victories, Soviet Russia is winning her objectives now in rapid-fire fashion. The victory in Indochina is Russia's greatest since the Communist victory in China.

The Communists conquered at the Geneva Conference. They succeeded in forcing France, one of the great Western powers, to sue for peace on Communist terms. The Geneva Conference made Communist China a major power in international affairs and recognized in Southeast Asia a new and powerful Communist state.

How was Communism able to win in Indochina? By the refusal of France to cut the bonds of colonialism, an act which alone could have converted an embittered colony into a loyal ally, as the United States had made of the Philippines a loyal ally by making it free. As a result, Vietnam was partitioned by the Geneva Agreement and

247

the Red Star mounted higher; there could be no other outcome.

If, as is not unlikely, all Vietnam goes Communist, Laos and Cambodia, its neighbors, cannot long remain free. And next door lie endangered Thailand, and Burma, Indonesia, and Malaya—all of these already infiltrated by scheming Communists.

The most shocking part of the tremendous Communist victory in Asia is this: *in all these victories not one Russian soldier has been killed.*

To date one hundred and forty-two thousand American boys were casualties in Korea—killed, wounded, and missing. They fought not merely to save that unhappy land, but to hold the defense line of the Pacific. They fought in Korea in order that their brothers may not have to fight in San Francisco, Chicago, and New York.

Chinese have been killed, and Koreans, and Filipinos, and Vietnamese. But not Russians! Russia fights by proxy and wins by proxy; the honors and the booty are Russia's alone.

Again with an eye on the map, let us consider the manpower that has fallen or may yet fall to Russia.

The Chinese and Koreans have fought Russia's war, while Russia's own tremendous manpower reserve remains untouched. Why should Russians fight! Russia has more than one billion people in Asia ready to fight its wars—one thousand million to send to death against the free world.

If Russia conquers all Asia and forces all Asia to fight for her, what will the tally be? Who will help Freedom fight its battles in Asia?

As the figures stand now, the forces of Freedom include

twenty-one million Filipinos, eighteen million Thailanders, and eighty million Pakistani. One hundred nineteen million in all. That is all we can count on at this time.

There are eighty million Japanese. I cannot with any conviction list them on the side of Freedom. They would be a powerful addition to our side, but how can we believe that an ancient imperialism like Japan has been democratized after seven short years of military occupation! Democracy has been imposed upon them since the end of World War II, yet one wonders whether they could have changed so much since then.

Suppose Japan had won and Tojo had been sent to Washington, instead of MacArthur to Tokyo, and the Japanese army of occupation were in control in every state and city of the Union. Can any American believe that in seven years he would have forgotten the tenets of the Declaration of Independence, the principles of the Constitution, the teachings of Washington, Jefferson, and Lincoln, and the ways of life to which he has been accustomed, and instead has come to believe in the divinity of the Emperor and in the entire fabric of feudal doctrine and custom that has sustained Japanese life for centuries? I do not think that any people can change so much in seven years. Why then do we expect the Japanese to change so suddenly, with his ancient civilization and his traditions set deep in antiquity?

When we discussed with John Foster Dulles in 1950 the issues of the Japanese Peace Treaty, the Philippine Government proposed that a system of education be established in Japan, under United Nations auspices, with emphasis on the teaching of the precepts of freedom and democracy. Mr. Dulles rejected this proposal. Today, Japan's leadership is divided between the Tojo-minded Zaibatsu and the new Communists—and the people do not know enough of democracy to remember the lessons of the first or to understand the perils of the second. They cannot resist the insidious propaganda being skilfully piped into their country from Russia.

No, I do not list the Japanese on the side of democracy. What have we left, then, in Asia? To repeat, one hundred and nineteen million Thailanders, Pakistani, and Filipinos.

These are all we can count on to stand against four hundred sixty million Chinese, and behind these is the untouched reservoir of two hundred million Russians.

The population of the United States is one hundred sixty million.

We must face the fact that the democratic forces are snowed under by Red numbers. We must realize also that Russia's actual attack against the free world is just beginning.

Japan had as its excuse for transgression the need for more living space. Japan's war was waged with the aid of hatred of the White Imperialist. Actually, Japan won its war, having won its point; the white man has been driven from Asia.

Russia's aim is deadlier: it is the physical and spiritual domination of the world.

The Filipinos, because they sided with freedom and democracy, were made to suffer brutalities and devastation by the Japanese. Yet that was only a foretaste of what Communism will do to the freedom-loving Filipinos if not stopped in time.

250

We know what is going on next door, inside Communist China. From unimpeachable sources we learn how Christian Chinese are being made to suffer in a land where no Christian church is left standing. We know of the systematic brutalization of young girls by party members, to break down their "bourgeois" training, and of the "brain-washings" given older people to rid their minds of the last vestiges of freedom and democracy.

Those who fail to conform are publicly executed. The young people are forced to stand by, watching, while the objectors are shot, Russian fashion, in the back of the head. It is not uncommon to see indoctrinated children dance and jeer before their "non-conforming" fathers and mothers while their parents' brains are blown out.

That is why the Soviets "permit" mothers to work, that the children may be crammed with Communist propaganda when safely away from the "softening" influences of home. Brutalize the babies and there will be no "softness," no "unreality" in the Communist hordes overrunning the future world.

This is the Communist dream. It has no place in a world of free men.

Twice, with our blood, we have held the Philippines. We defied Japan, we refused to yield to Communism. We are just ending our struggle against the Communist attack from within that was far more dangerous than the struggle that ended on Leyte.

We know this is not the end. When the full sweep of Communist aggression is carried out, we will again be in Russia's way. Now is the time to prepare, with all that is left of the free world, to hold every line against Soviet Russia that can possibly be held.

In my extensive travels around the United States I have noticed everywhere the unmistakable symptoms of panic. It is paradoxical and dangerous that the most powerful country in the world should give way to hysteria, for the hysterical are too easily stampeded through fear. That is the way Russia conquered in other lands—by stampede and by terrorism. They have now added a new element to their strategy—conquest by proxy. This is terrorism with finesse. When they have set all the rest of the world fighting, brother against brother, nation against nation, the Russians can sit back to wait for easy global victory. Then, perhaps, we shall see the iron-faced ones smile!

The Russian leaders are not only dedicated; they are cunning. Russia will fight to the last Korean, the last Chinese, the last Vietnamese, the last Filipino, and, if it has its way, to the last American.

Materialism! Realism! Despotism! These are the banner words of the Red Messiah.

Still, in the United States, I hear the blind-in-heart objecting: "So what! Why should we concern ourselves with anything going on in Asia? Why should we try to make friends over there? Let the Asians fight for Asia."

Americans should concern themselves *because this may be Freedom's and Democracy's last crusade.* To fail to understand this may result in turning Asia over to Soviet Russia.

The question is now: Will America stand by and see turned over to Russia all of Asia, with its terrifying potential, its teeming millions, its inexhaustible resources, its important raw materials? Can any American believe that his country can maintain its national security without allies, when a dozen bombs dropped tomorrow at certain vital areas can immobilize America? For a long time America was snugly protected on either side by the Pacific and the Atlantic oceans. But the oceans no longer afford protection against submarine and guided air power.

The isolationist is as the turtle in his shell, and the simile is doubly appropriate because the turtle is also slow to comprehend when he has been left helplessly kicking on his back.

Against a master Russia, swollen with the tremendous accrual of Asian manpower and material, can America survive?

Every American must already know the answer in his own heart. Lose Asia to Russia—and America is lost!

Chapter XV

THE situation in Asia is not hopeless. There still remains the great reservoir of the neutral or uncommitted peoples of Asia. These comprise approximately three hundred sixty million people of India, eighteen million Burmese, eighty million Indonesians, and eight million Ceylonese.

It is dangerous to oversimplify and to regard these uncommitted Asian countries as lost, in ideology if not in a military sense, to Communism, and thereby to be written off as a total loss to the free world.

In the face of all the "alienation of allies" talk, it is important to remember that the uncommitted peoples of Asia, while not actual allies of the United States, are still non-Communist countries. They have shown their profound hunger for peace. It is upon this longing for peace that Americans should build an understanding with the Asian peoples that will work for peace. The understanding must come from both sides of the Pacific if it is to be an effective force against Communism.

There are millions of the uncommitted in Asia who will side with democracy if America can gain their faith once more. They need the assurance of America's good will and an understanding of their aims and ideals that were so long ignored by the Western powers. Because that assurance has been withheld, they are not actively committed to our side.

How can they be committed to our side? Asia is flaring all over with little "hot wars." They end in temporary truces only to flare again. The cease-fire in Indochina went into effect on August 3, 1954. How long will it last?

There is trouble in British Malaya and Korea, and rumblings in Burma, India, and Indonesia.

Only in the Philippines are we mopping up the last of the Huk Communists. Our "hot war" is over. Why has this not happened elsewhere? Why have not Asian countries taken an equally firm stand against Communism?

The encouraging answer is that in countries such as Thailand, whose freedom was long respected, and the Philippines, to which independence was freely given, Communism has not been able to assume control. In other countries, where independence has been denied, or has been promised and then withheld, the Communists were able to capture the nationalist movement and use it for their own ends. Communism rode to power on the bandwagon of the so-called "national liberation movement."

To understand this we must consider honestly the relationship between America and Asia and the tragic lack of understanding on both sides of the Pacific.

I have given the side of the neutral Asian. He has been taught by Communist propaganda to bracket the American with all the other white overlords he has hated so bitterly and so long. Now he is no longer helpless; he thinks this is his chance to affiliate with a great and growing power, the Soviet Union, which is pledged to drive away colonial imperialism in Asia. He blinds himself to the Communist danger in order that he may have his revenge against the hated European imperialism.

On the other side of the Pacific is another and equally dangerous form of blindness. Many times, in the United States, I have found myself shouting a message of warning that few seem prepared to heed, and I have been made to feel as helpless as on those days in Manila when we shook our puny fists at the death-dealing bombers overhead that carried the emblem of the Rising Sun.

Everywhere, in a victorious, easygoing, and contented country, I heard Americans say of Asia: "That's on the other side of the world! Let the Asians do the fighting."

But Asia is no longer on the other side of the world. Russia is no longer made ineffective by distance, not with the new missiles; not while Russian guns are being shipped into countries next door to the Panama Canal; not while Communist infiltration is being skilfully practiced within the United States!

All my life I have been commuting between the United States and the Philippines. It was a long journey by boat when I was a youth going to school in America. Every year the distance has shortened, until now I commute by air, deciding in advance on breakfast in San Francisco one day and dinner the next day in my home in Manila, or dinner in San Francisco and breakfast a day later in Manila. Asia is no longer far away.

Still, in the United States, I have heard bitter comment: "Why should we send our boys to fight in Indochina? We aren't fighting any battles for Asians!"

America, child of revolution, seeing its revolutionary

inheritance handed on to Asia, cannot see it lost by default to Soviet Russia.

And on Asia's side there are questions asked that have not been answered. No one has taken the trouble to explain to the Asian what the real American policy is. He, too, hears the cry, "Save Asia." And he asks: From whom? For what? In whose interests? By what means? He is not going to offer up his poor life to save Asia from Communism, so that colonialism shall remain on his shoulders.

No one has told the Asian that the fight to hold Indochina was not a salvage operation for French colonial interests, but for freedom. For that matter, the American has not been told that, either.

America is on the defensive in Asia and misunderstanding is deepening between Asia and America because of errors made in dealing with Asia since World War II. As one example, the cry to save Indochina was always, "Aid France." Why? Because France is a key power in the Western Alliance. It occurred to nobody that a far better reason to save Indochina was, and is, to save the peoples of Indochina for freedom!

How can Asians not believe the Communist propaganda when America is placed in the unfortunate and unworthy position of upholding the colonial interests of its Western European allies? The clear line against imperialism of all stripes, whether Western or Russian, was not drawn in time. Now it may be too late.

There was the earlier example of the Indonesian struggle for independence. Everybody recognizes that this great nation of eighty million people would not have won its independence if the United States had not exerted pressure on the Dutch to set it free. Why, then, is Indonesia not siding whole-heartedly with America in the current cold war?

Part of the answer is to be found in the equivocal attitude of America at the beginning of the Indonesian struggle for freedom. America had been reluctant to displease the Dutch and to "weaken" the Netherlands as a member of NATO. In statement after statement in the Security Council I helped to champion the Indonesian cause as a representative of the Philippines. In private conversations with high American officials and in speeches before American audiences I warned that America's reluctance to support the Indonesian struggle was a betrayal of America's own revolutionary past and that America would be judged, in Asian eyes, by the company of the colonial powers which it preferred to keep. When, after much vacillation and spilling of blood in Indonesia, the United States eventually pressured the Dutch into relinquishing their hold on Indonesia, it was too late. By that time, the Indonesian people had begun to distrust America. Their minds had been poisoned by doubts while they waited and hoped, for meantime, Dutch soldiers, wearing uniforms made in America and using arms made in America, were carrying on a so-called "police action" against the Indonesian people.

If, in the beginning, the attitude of America toward Indonesia had been on the pattern of its generous attitude toward the Philippines, eighty million Indonesians would be with us today, committed on the side of the free world. If, in the beginning, the United States had stipulated that there would be a general liquidation of the colonial system in Asia, this would have sealed the trust of the Asian peoples.

America stands at the crossroads in Asia. On one hand is the American ideal, sprung from its revolutionary traditions, its record of liberating and recognizing the independence of the Philippines. On the other hand, political expediency inclined the United States to moderate its sympathy for the peoples of Asia and Africa so as not to alienate its Western allies, which include of course the colonial powers.

The commitments assumed by the United States under NATO made it no easy matter for America to support the colonial interests of its European allies and at the same time keep faith with Asia. The situation brought on a dangerous dilemma, made even more so by the Communist pretense that Russia is the only true foe of Western imperialism and the only true champion of the subject peoples. Millions in Asia and Africa have been subjected to such propaganda. If they were swayed by these arguments, it is not because they feared the new and little-known Communist imperialism the less, but because they hated more the centuries-old White imperialism they know too well. The recent talk of "aiding" the French in Indochina only gave support to the Communist claims.

We must bear in mind that the word "democracy" does not necessarily strike a responsive chord in the heart of every Asian. The pattern of Asian society from time immemorial has been, as a rule, authoritarian rather than democratic. Therefore we should not expect the great bulk of the Asian peoples to be filled with a passion for democracy, particularly since the Communists have cleverly taken over the term "democracy" by calling their dictatorial regimes "popular democracies." The fact is that democracy in the Western sense, based on the fundamental principle of the rights and freedom of the individual, has gained a foothold in only a few countries in Asia. The Philippines is one of these.

Since the surrender of Japan, the story of Asia is that of a continent struggling valiantly and without too much success to recover from a war foisted upon it by power-greedy aggressors. Asia was laid waste by Japan and left too prostrate and weak to resist or even to recognize the advance of a newer, more ruthless, and infinitely better-equipped aggressor looming in the West.

Even today the greater part of Asia seems unaware of the far more dangerous overlordship of Russia. The fact is that the Asian has been rendered deaf and blind to the Communist menace by his determination that the White Man shall not rule again. That determination has also been nourished by Communist propaganda.

It is this lack of awareness in Asia of the Communist danger—this apparent tendency to discount its significance compared to the domination of the white European from which Asia has just emerged—that presents the greatest danger today to freedom. It can be ascribed to the fact that the war, which produced its great partisan and military leaders in Asia, did not bring a new concept of leadership into being except in one country. The prewar leaders of Asia wrote a shining page of history, but they are still rehashing today the anti-colonial lessons they used to preach with such tremendous effect, and the lessons are outdated.

The exception to the over-all Asian picture is in the Philippines, where the conditions under which independence was achieved made it possible to shift emphasis from the struggle against the overlordship of the white man to the problems which a people, relieved of the necessity to fight anew for its political freedom, faced with the advent of that freedom.

If this American-Philippine method of instilling democracy at the lower levels had been followed in Japan, for example, who can say that Asia today would not be a freer continent, with a better awareness of the promise and the dangers of the future?

The new Russian propaganda centered on the so-called "peace offensive" makes it more urgent that the West, particularly the United States, continue to give assistance to the underdeveloped countries on a basis of self-help and mutual respect, and not as a special favor with political strings attached, nor as a disguised vestige of colonial imperialism.

Ever since the Atlantic Charter, which gave the false hope to Asia that it might benefit thereby, was signed at the beginning of World War II, I have been advocating a Charter for the Pacific based on a similar pattern. This became all the more necessary after Winston Churchill, one of the two co-authors of the Atlantic Charter, made it painfully clear to the non-self-governing peoples of Asia and Africa that the bright promise of that historical document was not meant for them. As a result, I outlined the blueprint for a Pacific charter in my book, *Mother America*, published before the founding of the United Nations. If such a pattern had been followed, much of the misunderstanding and confusion that has proved a fatal barrier to world peace might have been avoided.

The picture in Asia has changed radically since the Atlantic Charter was signed. But in view of what Churchill said, the changes took place in spite, and not because, of the Atlantic Charter. It became obvious that we should have a charter of freedom for the countries rimming the Pacific if the area was to be saved for democracy.

More than once has the olive branch of understanding been proffered across the Pacific by the Philippines, the meeting place for half a century between East and West.

In 1949 the Philippine Government proposed that the United States boldly assume leadership in establishing a defensive system for Southeast Asia in the same way that NATO already guaranteed the security of Western Europe. The suggestion was lightly passed over.

Despite America's indifference we insisted on our plan, and in 1950, at Baguio, our mountain capital, a conference which I had the privilege of organizing and over which I presided, was held, with official representatives of Australia, Ceylon, India, Indonesia, Pakistan, Thailand, and the Philippines. The meeting closed with the adoption of this principle: "That in the consideration of the special problems of South and Southeast Asia the point of view of the peoples of this area be prominently kept in mind, by any conference dealing with such problems, so that better understanding and cordial relations may subsist between the countries in the region and other countries of the world." This conference was virtually unnoticed by the American press.

Western leaders now recall rather wistfully that these appeals were voiced some time ago by peoples who longed to be understood by the greatest democracy in the world, but who went unheard. The plea was heard instead by Soviet Russia, which had plans of its own.

Five-power military talks between America, Great Britain, France, New Zealand, and Australia were held in 1952, 1953, and 1954 to discuss the defense of Asia against Communism. Why were Pakistan, the Philippines, and Thailand, the three Asian nations now in alliance with the West, not asked to join the discussions? Surely it would have been useful to invite to the meeting Lieutenant General Jesus Vargas, able and courageous Filipino field commander under President Magsaysay, who successfully fought the Communists in the field. None of those in the discussions actually fought them in the field as General Vargas did. Yet when the United States insisted on including the Philippines and Thailand in the talks, and Great Britain refused, America gave in. On what grounds we were excluded and denied the right to speak, we were never told.

But here, again, even in this relatively minor incident, we see the kind of dangerous blunder the United States is almost always certain to make so long as it permits its own Asian policy to be made in London or Paris instead of basing it courageously on its own historic traditions of liberty and on the pattern that it so wisely set in the Philippines.

To get closer to the heart of Asia, America must use its own heart more. The peoples of Asia will respond with understanding and sympathy to the freedom-loving, the generous-hearted, the deeply humane America of Washington, Jefferson, Lincoln, and Franklin Delano Roosevelt; on the other hand, nothing will more surely repel them than an America that carelessly allows its escutcheon to be blemished by the sins of its European allies.

Furthermore, it cannot be overemphasized that in the recent past the judgment on Asian questions as well as the Asian policy formulated by some of America's allies have proved disastrous.

Let us review the events that led to and followed the Manchurian conflict of 1931. It will be recalled that after a suitable incident had been started by Japan, the latter immediately undertook a major campaign for the conquest of Manchuria. The League of Nations dispatched the Lytton Commission in the hope of finding a peaceful solution. But the conquest of Manchuria was completed before the arrival of the Commission.

The United States, though not a member of the League, gave full support to the organization in its effort to end the conflict. Public opinion in the United States was virtually unanimous in denouncing the Japanese action as an act of aggression, and Secretary of State Henry L. Stimson based his policy on the system of collective security which rested on the League Covenant and on the Paris Peace Pact of 1928.

The Lytton Commission, however, thought differently. It made all sorts of excuses for the Japanese aggression, including the statement that "in Manchuria there are many features without an exact parallel in other parts of the world." While advocating an autonomous regime for Manchuria, it concurred in Japan's claim that Manchuria was its "life-line," and expressed concern that Japanese legitimate interests there would be safeguarded.

The Lytton Commission, of course, reflected the policy of Great Britain, which at that time had an alliance with Japan. Its action gave grounds for the belief that General Tanaka spoke the truth way back in 1927 when he said that Japan had sounded out the European powers and had secured from them the pledge of a free hand in Manchuria.

Thus, in Manchuria, started the chain of Japanese expansionism and aggression which in 1941, ten years later, culminated in the Japanese aggression against Southeast Asia.

What does this bit of history teach us? A great deal, if we are willing to learn. Substitute Korea and Indochina for Manchuria, and Communist China and Soviet Russia for Japan in this context—the other protagonists are the same—and the parallelism becomes startling indeed. New Lyttons we now have to placate the aggressor and to recognize the fruits of aggression. How can anyone believe that the results will be different this time and that the United Nations, by appeasing Communist China, will reap peace where the League of Nations reaped only the continuation of Japanese aggression?

If Secretary Stimson were still living, one wonders what he would say to the Lord Lyttons of today. Though Stimson is dead, the perceptive intelligence which enabled him to tag aggression and to oppose it from the beginning has not vanished. His spirit lives in those who have the courage to affirm the truth and to stand by the principles and purposes of the United Nations despite the inducements of political expediency and a false peace.

America should beware of the Lord Lyttons of 1955!

Chapter XVI

WE cannot overestimate the power of words. Communism has been planted all over the world by words carefully scattered, like evil seeds. The bitterness and resentment sown against the White Man are apparent in the Red harvest. Russian guns and Russian soldiers did not conquer. The real victor has been the power of the expressed Communist dream superimposed on fear, or rather the false presentation of that dream, since once it is accepted, it changes to nightmare. This we had to remember in planning a charter for the Pacific.

In Asia we had dreamed and hoped for such a charter since the Atlantic Charter was signed, when many of us were still under the Japanese heel. Since a charter is made up only of words, certain key words would be of paramount importance.

Japan then, and Russia now, had the magic-word hate-formula in: "Asia for the Asians!" In each case this was translated by these two aggressor nations to mean in turn "Asia for the Japanese," and "Asia for the Russians."

We needed a word powerful enough to turn the edge of the hate slogan. In the Philippines we have such a word. It was given us by America with the pledge of independence, half a century ago. It gained the full force of its power when we achieved that freedom. It was, and can be again, the strongest ally of the West in the Far East. It is the word "independence," which means the right to be free. That word enabled us to meet and defeat Communism in the Philippines.

Freedom, independence, democracy, were once synonymous terms in the Asian mind. They can be made so again, when mutual understanding is achieved between Asia and America. The Asian will believe in democracy again when he has proof that it is democracy and not White Imperialism under another name.

It was this not-altogether-unfounded suspicion that gave the Japanese cry of "Asia for the Asians" the power to launch the attack on Pearl Harbor. It was this same cry that Molotov and Chou En-lai voiced again in Geneva, and which turned more of Asia over to the Communists.

I also used that slogan, back in 1945 in San Francisco, during the founding of the United Nations. I used it then because I was fighting for democracy and for peace, and it was plain that the key struggle in the newly-founded United Nations would be that of imperialism versus independence in Asia. The right place to fight out this ancient contest was on the floor of the San Francisco Opera House. It was of utmost importance that the Charter should register the triumphant ideal of independence over colonialism. For this reason I determined to fight for the inclusion of the word "independence" in the chapter concerning non-self-governing territories in the United Nations Charter.

There were protests from the representatives of the

colonial powers. Britain, France, and the Netherlands wanted the word "self-government" used instead. They claimed it had the same meaning as the word "independence."

But as an Asian I knew these two words could never hold the same meaning in the Asian mind. At that time India, Burma, Ceylon, Pakistan, Indonesia, and the Philippines were still bound to the metropolitan countries and hoped to be set free. The peoples of these countries were still looking trustfully to America as the one great Western nation capable of understanding their longings.

The people of the metropolitan countries, the Americans, British, French, and Dutch, enjoyed independence and seemingly took their freedom for granted. To explain to their representatives at the founding Conference of the United Nations the needs and longings of what had always been considered only as a mass of dark, mysterious, inscrutable, and voiceless people, and in particular to focus American attention upon the importance of including in the Charter that one word, "independence," I too found the "Asia for the Asians" slogan advantageous and made full use of it at every opportunity during the founding of the United Nations.

Against the representatives of the colonial powers I argued that the term "self-government" did not fully express the hopes of the Asians, since self-government is only the stage that prepares the way for independence, and therefore the wording in the Charter must include both self-government and independence.

The contest was long and at times embittered, but I could not yield because I was deeply convinced of the need for the concept and reality of independence. In the effort to secure its inclusion I freely admitted many of the benefits and advantages that colonialism had given the people it rules, but that the time of colonialism had ended, just as the divine rule of kings had ended, and that in the evolution of humanity the right of any country to possess another had reached its end, and that the poorest government is better than a government that is not one's own.

The final fight for the inclusion of the word "independence" took place in the Trusteeship Committee. After I had won my debate with Lord Cranborne of the United Kingdom and left the floor, Harold Stassen sent over a penciled note: *Congratulations. We are proud of you.*

Present among the observers that day was the late Dr. Hamilton Holt, who had been at the Versailles Conference as advisor to President Wilson, and was at the time president of Rollins College in Florida. He introduced himself and offered an honorary degree from the college "for what you have accomplished here today."

The word "independence" is in the Charter of the United Nations. It is only a word, and it may not seem important to men who have lived all their lives as free men. But to millions in Asia, that word held then and holds still the hope of the eventual recognition of every human right. The slogan of "Asia for the Asians" had served its purpose in helping to secure that word for the Charter.

I used it the rest of that year to aid my fight for independence in Asia. The slogan served my purpose in Washington and in New York, on the floor of the Assembly, on lecture platforms, in interviews all over the United States, and in magazine articles and books.

In an article in *Collier's* entitled "Asia Must Be Free," I argued that Asia must be recognized as belonging to the Asians in the same way that America had established the Monroe Doctrine as a hands-off policy for the Western hemisphere.

All this was in 1945—the year of the founding of the United Nations.

I might have used that slogan again, five years later, when in 1950 as Secretary of Foreign Affairs I was one of the architects of foreign policy for the Philippines. I might have made it the central theme of our policy. But by that time nearly all the Asian nations held by the Western powers had been given their freedom and the slogan no longer had much meaning. I felt that to use it again at such a late date would place an obstruction on the United Nations struggle for world peace. Racial barriers are road-blocks in the way of democracy.

So instead of the "Asia for Asians" slogan I emphasized "nationalism," since that is the key word of Communism. By doing this we stole the thunder of the Reds.

The slogan now, as used by Molotov, Chou En-lai or other Communist representatives, can only be translated to mean "Asia for the Communists." It has a sinister connotation on their lips.

But the power of the word "independence" has grown, and today it is more important than ever before.

This was amply demonstrated at the time of the signing in September, 1954, of the Southeast Asia Collective Defense Treaty, otherwise known as the Manila Pact, and its accompanying fulfillment of our long dream, the Pacific Charter.

For twelve years, many Asians and many Americans (among the latter the late Wendell Willkie) had pressed the need for an agreement or Pacific Charter, to serve as defense against our common enemy in the Pacific. Nothing was done.

Now in April, 1954, came the evil news of Indochina and the fall of Dienbienphu. The Western powers knew at last, having been shown by the triumphant Communist representatives at the Geneva Conference, that the Communist tide in China could not be rolled back without launching World War III.

The time for defense had passed. All this time, the West had been on the defensive. The need now was to counterattack. The immediate need was to draw the line against Communism in the Far East, to stay Russia in its juggernaut advance toward the Pacific defense line.

Now was the time to draw the line in Asia marking the peril point: declaring that on this line democracy would fight, and that any incident or threat beyond the line by Soviet Russia would be considered an act of aggression against the forces of democracy. There was a moral right to draw this line in the Orient.

The meeting at Baguio in 1950, and subsequent meetings among Asian leaders, had given proof that there was in South and Southeast Asia an awareness of this need and a strong preference for the principles and institutions of freedom and democracy, as well as a tremendous reservoir of good will for the United States. It was to this

272

reservoir of good will and faith in democracy that the West turned during the Geneva crisis.

Early in April, 1954, Secretary of State Dulles proposed to President Magsaysay that a joint declaration be made by the United States of America and interested powers in Southeast Asia to serve notice on Soviet Russia that they were in unity and to give warning that any further aggression in that region would not be tolerated. This was virtually an acceptance by America four years later of the proposal sent from Baguio in 1950.

As special envoy of the President of the Philippines in Washington I was requested to transmit this proposal to my government. I radiophoned President Magsaysay and he agreed to sign a joint declaration. Here was our chance to ask for the Asian equivalent of the Atlantic Charter that had been for so long our hope in Asia.

The Filipinos knew the effect such a charter would have in other parts of Asia. We knew that in the minds of all Asians the problem of Indochina and all other invaded lands, in sum, the problem of all Asia, presented not a test of American military effectiveness, but a far more serious test of the *American faith* in freedom and democracy.

The Asian reservoir of good will and faith in democracy will not be kept filled by a show of military power. It has been clearly demonstrated that military power does not impress Asians—that it can, indeed, impress them in a negative way.

What can impress the Asian peoples is a readiness to keep in mind their point of view. That point of view is, basically, the desire to maintain their independence, to

273

assist others in achieving independence, and to preserve peace in their own countries, their own continent, and throughout the world.

This had to be considered in planning a Charter for the Pacific.

It would have to be made clear that the nations signing such a charter were for the freedom and independence of all peoples, including those of Asia. After all the fighting, the sacrifices, the lives lost, and the promises made— this pledge had not been made good. America still stood among the uncommitted. America, as the largest and most powerful of the democratic nations, held highest rank among the uncommitted in the eyes of Asia. This was a misunderstanding that had to be cleared away before such a charter could be made effective.

All this was in President Magsaysay's mind when Secretary of State Dulles made the formal proposal that a joint declaration to guarantee the security of Southeast Asia be made. President Magsaysay's reply, therefore, to the American representative was to the effect that while the Filipinos were willing to join in making such a declaration, the declaration should be the Asian equivalent of the Atlantic Charter. "What you are proposing," he said, "is not a political plan to cleave to in defiance of Communism."

He said this not because he had any reservation against signing, but because, as a successful fighter against Communism, he knew that the only way to defeat Communism in Asia or anywhere else was to give the people something to fight *for*, not merely to fight *against*.

On April 17, in another trans-Pacific radiophone conversation, President Magsaysay instructed me in Washington to inform the State Department that the Philippines was willing to join in a declaration to be issued by like-minded states as a warning against further Communist aggression in Southeast Asia, *provided* the declaration contained "an affirmation of the rights of all peoples to freedom and independence."

In a press statement issued that same day by President Magsaysay and released simultaneously in Manila and in Washington, he emphasized that "the joint declaration, to have maximum effectiveness, should approach as closely as possible the guarantees of the Atlantic Charter," and said in conclusion, "it should be the Asian equivalent of the Atlantic Charter."

So for the first time in history an Asian head of state proposed a Charter for the Pacific similar to the Atlantic Charter, and this proposal I duly transmitted to the State Department.

Four days later, on April 21, I took advantage of an invitation of the National Press Club of Washington to address its members and to appeal to the American people to support the stand taken by the President of the Philippines. My speech is reprinted at the end of this book. In this speech I emphasized the need to fire the imagination of the people of Asia with such a charter in order to convince them that America was not supporting colonialism but was for the freedom of the peoples of Asia.

After this speech, which was inserted in the Congressional Record and made the subject of an address on the floor of the United States Senate by Senator Thye of Minnesota, I carried the proposal across the continent on a speaking tour. I stressed the need of such a charter at the commencement exercises of Rockhurst College in Kansas City, where I was co-speaker with ex-President Truman and was given an honorary degree of Doctor of Laws. In Los Angeles, Portland, and Seattle, where I also received degrees, I stressed the need of the Pacific Charter, and at Knox College in Galesburg, Illinois, where I spoke on the spot where Lincoln once spoke, and sat in his chair. Speaking of the Charter for the Pacific on that spot, I felt his presence.

These speeches attracted attention and a great deal of editorial comment. They became the subject of a "debate" on the floor of the United States House of Representatives on June 9 when Congressman John W. McCormack of Massachusetts, Democratic minority floor leader, heartily endorsed the idea. His "opponent," the Republican Congressman Walter H. Judd of Minnesota, who is considered one of the outstanding American experts on Far Eastern affairs, supported McCormack, so what began ostensibly as a debate ended as a two-party endorsement of the Pacific Charter.

Senator Lehman of New York and Senator Kennedy of Massachusetts and others took up the cause of the Charter, so in ways both public and official, opinion in the United States was being turned to the Pacific Charter.

It was at this time when the Geneva Conference was proving to be a major Communist victory that Secretary Dulles proposed the holding of the SEATO Conference in Manila.

This title, standing for the Southeast Asia Treaty Organization, is a misnomer, and gave the Communists additional ammunition for the steady critical fire they poured on all our plans. To label the conference as Southeast Asian is misleading, since the United States, England, New Zealand, Australia, and France were represented, and none of these countries are in Southeast Asia. It is far more accurate to call it the Manila Conference, and the resulting treaty the Manila Pact.

Plans for the Manila Conference went ahead, and this seemed an opportune time to ask the United States to implement our Mutual Defense Treaty. The United States-Philippine Mutual Defense Treaty was between the two countries and had nothing to do with the Manila Pact. It is a military treaty which I had negotiated in 1951 when I was Secretary of Foreign Affairs, and signed in Washington. It is a guarantee that any attack on the Philippines would be considered a threat to the security of the United States and that in such an event the United States would act "in accordance with its constitutional processes."

This treaty, however, had never been properly implemented, and on May 25, 1954, as the result of a conference that I had with President Eisenhower on April 30, 1954, on instructions from Manila, President Magsaysay and Charles E. Wilson, the United States Secretary of Defense, agreed on the creation of a joint Philippine-United States council to implement this important agreement. Thus, two meetings were held in Manila in September.

On September 4, two days before the opening of the conference, the council met in Manila for the first time. It was composed of Secretary of State Dulles for the United States and Philippines Secretary of Foreign Affairs and Vice President Carlos P. Garcia. They discussed the responsibilities and obligations of their respective countries in case of aggression and implemented the 1951 Mutual Defense Treaty.

It was in this council meeting, which was entirely separate from the Manila Conference two days away, that Secretary Dulles made the historic statement that was by far the most far-reaching and important one uttered during the meetings in Manila.

Our Mutual Defense Treaty reads that an attack on one country will be considered an attack on the security of the other, and each will act in accordance with its "constitutional processes." Certain objectors had interpreted this as a watered-down version of the NATO provision, wherein it is stated that an attack on one country shall be considered an attack on all and shall bring about an immediate counterattack. Other critics had pointed out that, the NATO nations all being white, Americans were quite willing to act automatically in their mutual defense, while a threat to an Asian country would be treated "in accordance with constitutional processes," implying a slower process of deciding on retaliation and counterattack.

Some United States Senators had fought the NATO commitment on the ground that it was a usurpation of the power of Congress to declare war. So when our Mutual Defense Treaty was negotiated, much later, the State Department, fearing the same opposition, replaced the NATO concept of "automatic" counterattack with the milder term "constitutional processes."

This might have been a bitter disappointment to the Filipino group supporting the NATO wording. Instead it

278

became the greatest triumph of the two meetings, for Secretary Dulles had to make the special, historic announcement that an attack on the Philippines by an aggressor would bring about an "automatic" counterattack by the United States.

This was the important word we wanted. It made no difference that it was not in our Mutual Defense Treaty. The statement had been made in open council by the representative of the United States. It was formalized in an exchange of notes between the two governments. It placed our Mutual Defense Treaty on the same level with the North Atlantic Treaty.

Incidentally, it gave strength to President Magsaysay's position with the Filipino people and showed them how wise they had been to stay on democracy's side.

That one word—again a single word—outweighed many guns.

So when the Manila Conference opened two days later, to last four days (September 6–9), our delegates did not have to insist upon the NATO type of treaty with its concept of "automatic" counterattacks. We had been pledged that word, in advance, by America.

This was the way we had dreamed it, since the first attack was made by Japan. Here in Manila representatives of the great Western powers and three of Southeastern Asia were sitting together and discussing their common danger and planning the long-hoped-for Charter of the Pacific. Here were the Asian and the Western leaders working together over the blueprint for democracy, not in military alliance, but as the guardians of a freedom in which every representative played his role in equal partnership. Here was our pinpoint country of the Philippines able to voice all that it had learned through the long fight and the bitter sacrifice, and here was the United States sitting besides us as partner, advisor, and friend. Here was our reward—this equality and the right to speak on equal terms—which the Filipinos had won by fighting for democracy. We had reached the Manila Conference by way of the Death March on Bataan and the tunnel of Corregidor. For this, many generations of Filipinos had sacrificed, suffered, died.

I looked at leaders, white and brown, working together on the blueprint for democracy and imagined the war lords Malenkov and Molotov, Chou En-lai and Mao Tse-tung watching from the outside and ignored. What a triumph for freedom this Charter!

Here is the first draft of the Pacific Charter as proposed by President Magsaysay:

> The Foreign Ministers of Southeast Asia and of the United States
>
> *Desiring* to establish a firm basis for common action to maintain peace and security in Southeast Asia, in accordance with the purposes and principles of the United Nations,
>
> *Convinced* that common action to this end, in order to be worthy and effective, must be inspired by the loftiest principles of justice and liberty,
>
> *Do hereby proclaim* the adherence of their respective governments and peoples to the following principles:
>
> First, they uphold the principle of self-rule and the right of peoples to self-government and independence;
>
> Second, they are prepared to continue taking effective practical measures to ensure the progress of peoples towards self-rule and independence;

THIRD, they desire to collaborate fully with each other and with other countries of this region in the economic, social and cultural fields in order to bring about higher living standards, economic progress and social security;

FOURTH, they are determined to act jointly and severally to repel by every means within their power any attempt to subvert the freedom or to destroy the sovereignty and territorial integrity of the free and independent states of Southeast Asia.

This is the Philippine conception of a Charter for the Pacific, first announced publicly by President Magsaysay, on April 17, 1954, introduced by me in various parts of the United States on a lecture tour, supported now in the Manila Conference by Pakistan, Thailand, and the Philippines, and eventually hammered there into a shape acceptable to all, with the cooperation of the "colonial" powers, France, Australia, and the United Kingdom, with the United States and New Zealand acting as mediators.

The final text of the Pacific Charter is as follows:

The Delegates of the United States, Great Britain, France, Australia, New Zealand, Pakistan, Thailand and the Philippines,

Desiring to establish a firm basis for common action to maintain peace and security in Southeast Asia, and the Southwest Pacific,

Convinced that common action to this end, in order to be worthy and effective, must be inspired by the highest principles of justice and liberty,

Do hereby Proclaim:

FIRST, in accordance with provisions of the United Nations Charter, they uphold the principle of equal rights and self-determination of peoples, and they will earnestly strive by every peaceful means to promote self-government and to secure independence of all countries whose peoples desire it and are able to undertake its responsibilities;

SECOND, they are each prepared to continue taking effective practical measures to insure conditions favorable to the orderly achievement of the foregoing purposes in accordance with their constitutional procedures;

THIRD, they will continue to cooperate in economic, social and cultural fields in order to promote higher living standards, economic progress and social well-being in this region;

FOURTH, as declared in the Southeast Asia Collective Defense Treaty, they are determined to prevent or counter by appropriate means any attempt in the treaty area to subvert their freedom or to destroy their sovereignty or territorial rights.

This is the Pacific Charter, a historic document which by pledging the colonial powers to withdrawal and to the granting of freedom to peoples not self-governing is the final and clinching repudiation of Communist charges against the West. Made after a decade of constant Communist aggression and constant retreat on the part of the ebbing forces of democracy, it is really the first diplomatic offensive taken against Communism in Asia. It is the most devastating answer that has been given to the Communistic lies by the free world.

This Charter if faithfully carried out will defeat Communism in Asia because its elements are hope, understanding, and faith—elements that are certain death to the Communist ideal.

The Manila Pact for mutual defense to halt aggression, which was drawn up in Manila, approved and signed by the eight nations, was based on mutual defense, economic cooperation and the moral principles laid down in the Pacific Charter. (See the end of the book for a copy of the treaty.) Its foundation *is* the Pacific Charter.

The Manila Pact was the third of the regional collective-security agreements concluded since World War II. The first two, NATO and the Treaty of Rio de Janeiro, were made between states in Europe and the two Americas which had been linked for two centuries by tradition, culture, and history.

There were no such ties between the European world and Asia. Beyond our fifty—often turbulent—years of the American rule in the Philippines, we who met in Manila had no common bonds. We were drawn together by an unsentimental sense of mutual danger to our freedom and our lives. So the Manila Pact is an advance over NATO and Rio.

We were piecing out the pattern for freedom in Manila. Freedom from fear. Freedom from want. Freedom from the Communist terror. Freedom from aggression, in any form, by any country. Guarantees were made in good faith, by eight separate and dissimilar countries, that an offense against one be considered an offense to all.

This in sum is the purpose of the Manila Pact, which, together with the Pacific Charter, was the beginning of democracy's counterattack against Communism.

Our conference was not without recognition from Moscow. All through the days that the Treaty and the Pact were being discussed in Manila, an intensive bombardment was being carried on by the Communists against Quemoy, an island seventy miles off the Chinese mainland. Evidently it was intended as preparation for an attack on Formosa. This was typical Communist timing, calculated to intimidate such countries as Thailand and the Philippines which lie in the path of Communist aggression in Southeast Asia.

In exactly the same fashion the Communists had timed the fall of Dienbienphu with the Geneva Conference. It was calculated to intimidate the delegates there, and it did. As a result, Communist China took over the Conference with high hand, and the thoroughly cowed democratic forces were forced to sue for a dubious peace. The Indochina truce signed in July was Russia's greatest victory. Gains present and future for the Communists were piled up at Geneva. It is impossible to know how much harm was done there to the side of freedom.

When a political conference is being held and a military operation is being carried out at the same time, democracy is likely to be left voiceless. That was the way it had been done in Geneva. But in Manila we stood our ground.

Publication of the Manila Pact in the world press brought a screech of protest from the Soviet Foreign Ministry. On September 14 official criticism of the Manila defense agreement was broadcast over the Moscow radio.

I should like to quote that statement in full but it is many thousands of words too long. Faithful followers of the Communist line and viewers and listeners on radio and television who have heard the Soviet line for years will know its arguments in advance and judge its claims according to their own beliefs. For my part, it affects me as Vishinsky's statements did on a day we convened in the United Nations with a wild hope of achieving a peace pledge from Russia, and heard instead a series of prattling remarks about the Russians being the only "true lovers of peace." It was unbelievable, that speech by Vishinsky in the hours when we were facing what seemed to be certain war. The text of the Moscow statement is equally unbelievable. We of the democracies and the Communists face two ways. We cannot see things the same way.

Among other charges, the Communists said the Manila Conference was in itself an act of aggression. (Russia considers anything that strengthens the aims of peace an aggression against Russia.) The Manila Pact, according to the Soviet Foreign Ministry, served "to aggravate the international situation" and was a "menace to the security of Communist China."

The conference, it was charged, had been organized "on the initiative and under the pressure of the U.S.A., and under the pretext of defending the countries of Southeast Asia against Communism." Under this pretext, "intensive preparations have been made for the forming of a new aggressive military bloc in that area." We of the Philippines only wish that part were true! No proviso has been made to back the Manila Pact with arms.

The Soviet diatribe filled seven columns of fine print in the New York *Times*. It blasted the "United States-initiated" Pact as an aggressive military bloc directed against "all the countries of Asia in general and against China in particular." It wound up with the stern admonition:

> The Soviet Government cannot consider the conference in Manila and the signing of the treaty on the defense of Southeast Asia otherwise than actions directed against the interests of security in Asia and the Far East and at

the same time against the interests of freedom and national independence of the peoples of Asia.

States-initiators of the creation of the mentioned new military bloc in the area of Southeast Asia and the Pacific take upon themselves the entire responsibility for actions which are in gross contradiction to the tasks of strengthening peace.

In the sharp repartee brought on between Russia and the United States by the signing of the Pact, Secretary of State Dulles had the final word. In his report on the Treaty to the American people he termed the Communist charges as "tragically revealing of their ambitions."

Both the Manila Pact and the Pacific Charter are in themselves a refutation of Soviet Russia's accusations which are based, as always, on the most plausible and yet palpable lies.

To begin with, Pact and Charter were not "initiated" primarily by the United States. The Asians who signed were not the dupes of a group of conniving Western powers determined to "perpetuate colonialism in Asia," as the Communists claim is the purpose of the Manila Treaty.

In 1950, during the Southeast Asia Conference at Baguio, an important principle had been established when the nations meeting there passed the unanimous resolution that when matters relating to Asia were discussed by the Big Powers, the Asian nations concerned should be consulted.

It was at Baguio that we first proposed, and were disappointed in not achieving, a pact for the Pacific, and a pledge of democracy for Asia. Now, four years later, the precepts implanted at Baguio provided the basis of the Manila Conference.

In Manila, in 1954, Asians with new equality and with equal voice conferred and signed a Treaty and a Charter with representatives of the United States, the United Kingdom, and France; so far had we advanced along the way of democracy. This meeting showed our fellow Asians that the way to equality is not by sitting with crossed feet contemplating the lotus.

Against the Communist lie that the Treaty was planned to perpetuate colonialism, we need point only to the principles in the Pacific Charter providing for self-determination and for economic progress as the means to defeat Communism.

Refuting the "act of aggression" claims made by the Communists against the Manila Pact are its palpable truths. It is defensive in purpose, aimed only at actual aggression, and provides for action to be taken against subversive action.

But of even greater importance than the Manila Treaty is the Pacific Charter. Before the Conference was held in Manila, certain neutral leaders in Asia referred contemptuously to Thailand, Pakistan, and the Philippines as mere "puppets" of the colonial powers, and prophesied that we would let these powers dictate to us in the conference since we lacked the "courage and guts" to speak for ourselves and for Asia. The conference itself was referred to as a hocus-pocus device intended to perpetuate colonialism in Asia under the mask of good will, and these charges, Communist-inspired, had cast a great deal of doubt over the areas containing the millions of "uncommitted" peoples of Asia who are still neutral.

In answer to these charges, the Pacific Charter offered by President Magsaysay was like a flag of freedom being raised again over ground considered lost, and it is in many ways most significant in Asian minds than the Treaty itself.

The Asian delegates had firm ideas of what they considered to be right and necessary, and were not slow in making their wishes known. The original draft of the Preamble of the Treaty read that the signatures of the representatives were desired "to strengthen the fabric of peace." The Filipinos insisted that two more words be inserted, so that the line read "the fabric of peace *and freedom*." They also insisted that a new article be inserted to pledge all the signatories to the "freedom and independence of the peoples of Asia."

These are our victories in the Manila Conference—words written by Filipinos in their own blood. "Freedom . . . self-determination—independence."

These gains proved to the rest of Asia that we are not puppets. We had asserted ourselves in the conference. We had shown that the Western powers were not dictatorial but that they came to Manila with open minds. They had shown their belief, and had underwritten that belief, that to fight Communism successfully, all colonialism must come to an end. So on the flag hoisted at Manila by President Magsaysay we can read those tremendously important words: *Freedom . . . independence . . . self-determination.*

These words we can point out to the so-called neutrals,

the "uncommitted," and to the Communists, who have refused to believe that White Men would ever underwrite such promises in Asia.

We can say, too: Such things are not achieved by sitting back with folded arms! Equality can be won only by those who are willing to stand on their feet and face as equals their fellow men. We in the Philippines earned the right to be equal and free when we defeated Communism and stayed on democracy's side, and we sat face to face with the great white powers in Manila.

Chapter XVII

AS I write this I am again in the United States, and I find that many Americans believe the world crisis to be over. For the first time since the Japanese invaded Manchuria almost a quarter century ago, there are no war headlines in the American press that directly concern America. To many this seems a time to relax and enjoy peace.

It may be wise to remember that the Communists never relax. They plan best and prepare most between wars.

Now is the time to perfect the political, economic, and military plan to counterattack Communism, if democracy is to be saved.

A vital point in the political phase of such a plan is that the United States must win, or in certain cases retain, the friendship of the non-Communist peoples of Europe, Asia, and South America that are not already bound to the United States by treaties of mutual defense and security.

The imperative need now is to commit them irrevocably to the side of democracy, that America may not be left as its own final outpost, beleaguered by a relentless enemy that will leave America powerless, no matter how many defenses from within she may devise.

The proffers of friendship I have cited from Asia to America should convince the Americans that there is no reason for cynicism or despair in attacking the problem of the "uncommitted" peoples of Asia. The Asian signatories of the Pacific Charter have given proof of the way their peoples feel.

The great enemy to peace in Asia—which in time must mean world peace—is not Communism. It is colonial imperialism. The free Asian countries and those which won independence since World War II—Thailand, India, the Philippines, Pakistan, Burma, Ceylon, Indonesia, and South Korea—are not committed to Communism. On the contrary, all are fighting Communism from within.

The Manila Pact and the Pacific Charter place three of these Asian countries on democracy's side. These should prove to millions of resentful and reluctant Asians that democracy has taken its final stand against imperialism in any form, and that the last vestiges of colonialism will go. Millions of Asians who have been on the verge of accepting Communism, hitherto unknown to them, over the colonialism which they have known and hated, now have proof that democracy is really democracy, and that Communism is only the hated colonialism in a new and more terrible form. With others, the reluctance is still due to the belief, which only the activation of the Pacific Charter can remove, that to side with the United States is to side with colonialism.

Another reason behind the reluctance of many of these peoples to commit themselves is that they believe that if they side with either the United States or Soviet Russia they will be pushing the world toward World War III.

My explanation of Nehru's refusal to place India on the side of the democracies is this: The Indians know that America will never attack them, and that America is in fact incapable of a sneak attack. But they cannot be sure of such restraint on the part of Soviet Russia, which is India's next-door neighbor. One of the grim advantages of a dictatorship such as Russia is that the dictator can order a sneak attack at midnight and another country is ruined permanently by morning. No democratic leader has such power.

The same explanation may apply to Burma, Ceylon, and Indonesia. They, too, are part of the neutral wall standing between the democracies and Soviet aggression.

It was a disappointment to many, including myself, that the Manila Pact did not provide for more definite military planning to repel Communist aggression. It expressed determination to resist aggression in the treaty area, but it created no military machinery with which to repel such aggression (despite the blatant accusations by Russia that that had been done!). I should like to see specified units kept on the alert by the free nations to deal at any time with Communist acts of aggression in Asia, and impetus given the program for training native armies in Asian countries to defend their countries from Communist attack either from outside or from within.

Added to Communist armed aggression, and a far greater danger, is the Communist policy in support of the promotion of international trade, and of participating in the United Nations programs of economic and technical aid to help raise the standards of living of the underdeveloped countries. The competition for the minds of the

Asian peoples now definitely includes a competition for their stomachs, their desire for material well-being.

It would not entail too great a sacrifice on democracy's side to make the hideously depressed areas of Southeast Asia an economic show window for the world, as the Philippines was made a political show window for Asia by the United States. I realize this seems like a harsh suggestion to offer America, which finds itself surrounded everywhere by starving faces and outstretched palms. But to develop key countries about to yield to Communism because they are poverty-ridden and starving; to loan them economic and agricultural experts; to enable them to have power plants and agricultural machines instead of guns—this is a small price for democracy to pay in exchange for the peace and freedom of Asia.

There is another major point in the plan to stop the Communist advance that needs to be mentioned. The Communist campaign of hatred for all whites has had much success. But when in Manila white leaders and brown sat together and with equal voice worked out the Pacific Charter and the Manila Pact, much of the poison in that hate was drawn.

More was drawn by the unanimous decision of the United States Supreme Court holding that segregation in schools, due to color, was unconstitutional. That decision has had a galvanizing effect in Asia and Africa.

The propaganda against white supremacy had provided Communism with its strongest ammunition. Always, when a Russian delegate spoke in the United Nations concerning the American claim to democracy, the opening attack was a sneering, "But what about their Negro problem?

How can you say America believes in freedom and equality when Negroes are discriminated against?" This argument has been weakened by the anti-segregation verdict. Once more the democratic, the Christian, word had proved more powerful than any bomb. It is a telling example of the way America can successfully wage its own crusade against Communism.

America has every right and need to repel Communist aggression, from the outside or from within. She has also the moral right and the need to quell hysteria within her own boundaries, and not to replace vigilance with panic.

The hysteria of fear against Communism has been engendered, first, by politics, since it serves the purpose of a few politicians to appear before their constituents as fighters against Communism; and second, by business, because it serves certain business elements to blame every slump and strike on Communism. Either method makes for misunderstanding and panic.

These were the tactics that served Hitler and his inner circle when they persecuted the Jews, with resulting national distrust and demoralization inside Germany, and of neighbor turned against neighbor.

Panic has nothing to do with a cautious and effective defense against Communism. To fail to recognize the insidious disease of Communism does not make it less dangerous, but to accentuate panic and distrust doesn't either.

America does need, however, to sell a recognition of her own greatness to Americans and to the rest of the world. It is inconceivable that the greatest nation in the world today should have sold itself short to so many. All over the world there is criticism, skilfully leveled against America by the Communists and their sympathizers, and no answers are given and no defense is made. Her nearest neighbors are being fed the poison of hatred and contempt for America. America, grand-master of advertising, is not trying hard enough to sell itself.

Only the blind will say that America has no need to propagandize itself, since it is the world's most powerful nation. America has made of advertising a science, an art, and a tremendous source of private wealth. Why not use some of that talent on America? Why not brief American tourists before they visit other countries, as American boys were briefed before entering foreign countries, during the war? Why not give official recognition to the power of good will that can put an end to the cheap Communist propaganda being directed so carefully, so steadily, to such countries as Mexico and Guatemala, next door to the United States? Why not pipeline some of America's great power to develop respect and good will into Asia?

When Fil-Americans were trapped like rats in the tunnel on Corregidor, our dying President Quezon sent a final command from that tunnel to our soldiers fighting on Bataan.

"You must hold, and hold, and hold."

I have heard those words in my own mind many times since then. The Philippines was conquered by Japan, but the Filipinos did not cease to fight. The Philippines was infiltrated by Russian agents and Russian propaganda, but the Filipinos held.

We fought our fight from the inside. Russian invasion may next come to us from the outside, if other countries fall. In that dread event, once more, we will try to hold. Can we, if the rest of Asia goes?

I am not decrying the danger. I have stood too close to the Communist threat to want one iota of vigilance to relax. Democracy must be every minute on the alert.

This we have learned from the Filipino fight for freedom—that we can fight Communism and preserve democracy only where the citizens of the country possess two attributes: vigilance and the willingness to sacrifice.

When a nation is alert, when it has men ready to come forward to meet danger in the moment of need—then only can a country remain free.

I have written this story of a new and tiny struggling Republic's victory over Communism because it offers the best evidence so far of what can be done to fight Communism from within. Ours was a fight waged and won by the people themselves. Not with guns, planes, or atom bombs, but with free ballots and with faith in freedom was Communist infiltration and subversion stopped in the Philippines.

Which is to say, by democracy!

Our fight against Communism which ended with the surrender of Huk Supremo Luis Taruc has in it certain basic lessons which may be applied for use against Communism in any country in the world. Yes, even in America, where Americans do not need to be resold democracy! It is not new to them. They have possessed it since 1776.

But faith in democracy must be continually fed, and the

spirit of democracy kept in constant action, if Communism is to be stopped in its attempt to take the world.

Before the Filipinos defied Communism they had to be recharged with faith in democracy, which had been lost to them by postwar confusion and greed.

When our government was weak and incompetent and graft-ridden, the people lost faith. They protected Taruc. They found excuses for Communism.

When the government changed and the Filipinos elected their own President, and were made to realize that intelligence and honesty had taken public office, from that day on they refused to hide Taruc. They turned against Communism. They fought for democracy.

The final victories of our crusade are the Manila Pact and the Pacific Charter.

These are the basic elements of that crusade:

Cut the navel cord that joins the subversive groups to the masses and the subversives cannot exist. Clean out graft and incompetence from the government—the filth Communism feeds upon—and Communism cannot survive.

Try it elsewhere—in Asia—in Europe—in America. It will work anywhere. It will be as effective on a world scale as it was in the Philippines.

People will fight for freedom when they have a stake in that freedom.

So before military alliances are formed between nations, the people themselves must first be inspired with the principles for which they are to fight.

One United States Congressman said to me when I was President of the United Nations General Assembly:

"You can't fight Communism with words."

No, not perhaps with mere words. But by building faith through the enunciation of certain unassailable moral principles, it can be done.

We saw it done—in the Philippines!

Afterword

THIS I envision for Asia:

A mighty continent that has found its soul at last, after a period of revolutionary upheaval.

Having broken the mold of its ancient civilization, it is feverishly at work to fashion a new way of thinking and living for its numerous children in the atomic age.

Rejecting both the materialism that would utterly change its basic spiritual drive and the anachronism that would throw it back to a lost and forgotten age, Asia faces the future sure of itself, unafraid.

Asia will decide the course which human history will take in the next millennium.

Asia will cast the deciding vote between Freedom and Communism.

It is for America of the present day to decide whether Asia will be a partner or an enemy in the great task that lies ahead for all the human race.

Appendix A

In the speech made before the National Press Club in Washington, D.C., on April 21, 1954, General Romulo said in part:

President Magsaysay won fame among our people as a fighter for the freedom and security of his country, first against the Japanese invaders and later against the Huks. Therefore, as President, he may be expected to be uncompromising in the pursuit of these objectives. Nevertheless, when he says, as he does in his latest statement on the Indochina situation, that the political element of that problem is of great concern to the Philippines as an Asian nation, he does so not out of mental reservation but out of a clear understanding of the basic issues that are involved in the conflict.

The conflict in Southeast Asia involves not merely rich lands and strategic territories. It involves human beings and their God-given aspirations to a better life in larger freedom. President Magsaysay, therefore, recognizes that Philippine participation in any joint action against the Communist threat in Indochina must have as powerful a justification as the relentless campaign which is being pursued at home under his personal direction against the internal enemies of the country's freedom and security. If, as may eventually be necessary, such joint action should require direct military cooperation, then it must be made clear to the Filipino people that such action is being undertaken not merely against something but for something, namely, the right of the Indochinese peoples to freedom and independence.

The tradition and history of the Filipino people would require this political motivation as a necessary precondition for the united action that is contemplated in Southeast Asia. I think it is true to say that this would be equally true of the American people, whose own traditions of liberty cannot allow them to ignore the fundamental right of self-determination which lies at the heart of the Indochina conflict.

It has been said that there is need for an Asian equivalent of NATO in Europe. The comparison is based on what appear to be considerations of a strictly military character. President Magsaysay has made what is undoubtedly a most pertinent observation regarding this proposal. While recognizing the importance of arrangements that might be made to insure the military security of the region, he has introduced the political element which alone can give meaning to any security arrangements in Southeast Asia. Instead of invoking NATO, he has gone somewhat farther back in history to invoke the Atlantic Charter. He is thus the first statesman to refer to a document which enshrined the ideals of the Allied Powers of World War II and to insist that those ideals be made applicable to Asia.

The four freedoms which were guaranteed under the Atlantic Charter are not a dead letter. In the context of the struggle in Asia they possess startling relevance. This is especially true when it is recalled that Winston Churchill had made it plain that the Atlantic Charter did not apply to Asia. It is fitting that the head of state of the first Asian country to achieve freedom after World War II should invoke the principles of the Atlantic Charter as the pillars which must support and sustain the contemplated united action of the free states of Asia and Europe against Communism. In effect, what President Magsaysay is saying to America and to the West is this: "In order to defend Southeast Asia against the Communist menace, we need not only the armaments and the manpower

302

which could be established under a Pacific NATO, but also the principles and the faith which can only be aroused by the reiteration of the four freedoms of the Atlantic Charter."

I stress these two statements on a burning international topic of the day because it shows Ramón Magsaysay in a new light and it throws into bold relief what the new look in the Philippines really is. Here is a man of the people, one who sprung from the masses, who, with his native intuition and unalloyed patriotism, senses an imminent danger to his country. He did not pussyfoot. He acted. He knows that his country cannot be secure with the forces of Communism on the rampage in Asia. And as one of the first truly Asian leaders, he is of pure Malayan stock, elected overwhelmingly in an uncontaminated popular election, he strikes at the root of the Asian revolution and speaking for the masses whence he came proposes the equivalent of the Atlantic Charter for Asia.

You once had a President here in Washington who also came from the people, who took over at a critical time, when the head of the Nation had to be an expert in international affairs as well as in domestic problems. Your history readings will tell you that that man, in his study just up the street, was not highly regarded by the so-called cultured statesmen of the day because he came from the people. Yet America was saved, at home and abroad, by that man, who applied to his task the great touchstone of what the people wanted—and of what he as a man of the people knew that the people wanted. Abraham Lincoln did not govern by what was accepted as the book of government. Lincoln fought and led the fight against disunion because he saw the danger to the Nation and to the people in disunion. He saved America.

On a smaller stage, yet one just as significant, Magsaysay is fighting for the salvation of his people. The issue as he sees it is not the danger of disunion, or only partly that. It is the disrupting influence of international Communism that Magsaysay sees as the great problem, the major threat to his people —because he has fought the Communists and he knows what they want, and what their program means. His devotion to the basic principle of serving the people is closely linked with his conviction that Communism constitutes the greatest threat to the people. As he sees the problem in an unorthodox way, so he tackles his solutions. Like Lincoln, or should I say, after the manner of Lincoln, he is not governing by the book. He writes his own book, and in doing so he gives democracy a deeper meaning, a stronger implementation.

Appendix B

The Parties to this Treaty,

Recognizing the sovereign equality of all the Parties,

Reiterating their faith in the purposes and principles set forth in the Charter of the United Nations and their desire to live in peace with all peoples and all governments,

Reaffirming that, in accordance with the Charter of the United Nations, they uphold the principle of equal rights and self-determination of peoples, and declaring that they will earnestly strive by every peaceful means to promote self-government and to secure the independence of all countries whose peoples desire it and are able to undertake its responsibilities,

Desiring to strengthen the fabric of peace and freedom and to uphold the principles of democracy, individual liberty and the rule of law, and to promote the economic well-being and development of all peoples in the treaty area,

Intending to declare publicly and formally their sense of unity, so that any potential aggressor will appreciate that the Parties stand together in the area, and

Desiring further to coordinate their efforts for collective defense for the preservation of peace and security,

Therefore agree as follows:

ARTICLE I

The Parties undertake, as set forth in the Charter of the United Nations, to settle any international disputes in which they may be involved by peaceful means in such a manner that international peace and security and justice are not endangered, and to refrain in their international relations from the threat or use of force in any manner inconsistent with the purposes of the United Nations.

ARTICLE II

In order more effectively to achieve the objectives of this Treaty, the Parties, separately and jointly, by means of continuous and effective self-help and mutual aid will maintain and develop their individual and collective capacity to resist armed attack and to prevent and counter subversive activities directed from without against their territorial integrity and political stability.

ARTICLE III

The Parties undertake to strengthen their free institutions and to cooperate with one another in the further development of economic measures, including technical assistance, designed both to promote economic progress and social well-being and to further the individual and collective efforts of governments toward these ends.

ARTICLE IV

1. Each Party recognizes that aggression by means of armed attack in the treaty area against any of the Parties or against any State or territory which the Parties by unanimous agreement may hereafter designate, would endanger its own peace and safety, and agrees that it will in that event act to meet the common danger in accordance with its constitutional processes.

Measures taken under this paragraph shall be immediately reported to the Security Council of the United Nations.

2. If, in the opinion of any of the Parties, the inviolability or the integrity of the territory or the sovereignty or political independence of any Party in the treaty area or of any other State or territory to which the provisions of paragraph 1 of this Article from time to time apply is threatened in any way other than by armed attack or is affected or threatened by any fact or situation which might endanger the peace of the area, the Parties shall consult immediately in order to agree on the measures which should be taken for the common defense.

3. It is understood that no action on the territory of any State designated by unanimous agreement under paragraph 1 of this Article or on any territory so designated shall be taken except at the invitation or with the consent of the government concerned.

ARTICLE V

The Parties hereby establish a Council, on which each of them shall be represented, to consider matters concerning the implementation of this Treaty. The Council shall provide for consultation with regard to military and any other planning as the situation obtaining in the treaty area may from time to time require. The Council shall be so organized as to be able to meet at any time.

ARTICLE VI

This Treaty does not affect and shall not be interpreted as affecting in any way the rights and obligations of any of the Parties under the Charter of the United Nations or the responsibility of the United Nations for the maintenance of international peace and security. Each Party declares that none of the international engagements now in force between it and any other of the Parties or any third party is in conflict with

307

the provisions of this Treaty, and undertakes not to enter into any international engagement in conflict with this Treaty.

ARTICLE VII

Any other State in a position to further the objectives of this Treaty and to contribute to the security of the area may, by unanimous agreement of the Parties, be invited to accede to this Treaty. Any State so invited may become a Party to the Treaty by depositing its instrument of accession with the Government of the Republic of the Philippines. The Government of the Republic of the Philippines shall inform each of the Parties of the deposit of each such instrument of accession.

ARTICLE VIII

As used in this Treaty, the "treaty area" is the general area of Southeast Asia, including also the entire territories of the Asian Parties, and the general area of the Southwest Pacific not including the Pacific area north of 21 degrees 30 minutes north latitude. The Parties may, by unanimous agreement, amend this Article to include within the treaty area the territory of any State acceding to this Treaty in accordance with Article VII or otherwise to change the treaty area.

ARTICLE IX

1. This Treaty shall be deposited in the archives of the Government of the Republic of the Philippines. Duly certified copies thereof shall be transmitted by that government to the other signatories.

2. The Treaty shall be ratified and its provisions carried out by the Parties in accordance with their respective constitutional processes. The instruments of ratification shall be deposited as soon as possible with the Government of the

Republic of the Philippines, which shall notify all of the other signatories of such deposit.

3. The Treaty shall enter into force between the States which have ratified it as soon as the instruments of ratification of a majority of the signatories shall have been deposited, and shall come into effect with respect to each other State on the date of the deposit of its instrument of ratification.

ARTICLE X

This Treaty shall remain in force indefinitely, but any Party may cease to be a Party one year after its notice of denunciation has been given to the Government of the Republic of the Philippines, which shall inform the Governments of the other Parties of the deposit of each notice of denunciation.

ARTICLE XI

The English text of this Treaty is binding on the Parties, but when the Parties have agreed to the French text thereof and have so notified the Government of the Republic of the Philippines, the French text shall be equally authentic and binding on the Parties.

UNDERSTANDING OF THE UNITED STATES OF AMERICA

The United States of America in executing the present Treaty does so with the understanding that its recognition of the effect of aggression and armed attack and its agreement with reference thereto in Article IV, paragraph 1, apply only to communist aggression but affirms that in the event of other aggression or armed attack it will consult under the provisions of Article IV, paragraph 2.

In witness whereof, the undersigned Plenipotentiaries have signed this Treaty.

Done at Manila, this eighth day of September, 1954.